COMMANDO TACTICS for DIGITAL FILMMAKERS

Creative Production Tips & Strategies

to Make Your Next Film or Video Shoot Successful

by

Craig D. Forrest

Published by Windsock Press

ISBN: 0615495478
ISBN-13: 978-0615495477

DEDICATION

To Andrew & Anneke, incredible son and daughter, who allowed Dad time away from home to see the Big Blue Marble.

To Rebecca, the most beautiful woman in the world...and mi amour. Thanks for truly loving and believing in this traveler.

ALSO BY CRAIG D. FORREST

The Influence of Alexander Mackendrick on the Kailyard Film Sub-Genre

TABLE OF CONTENTS

Acknowledgements

There are more than a few people I'd like to thank for their kindness, direction, friendship and humor over my television and documentary career.

Nothing would have happened if not for the creative guru, Roger Flessing, who gave a twenty year kid his first start in television.

A wonderful boss, Don Maynard, sent me out to travel the world, mistakes and all.

The best client - and colleague in the world - Ed Nelson, gave me my first contract, and remained supremely confident I'd get past customs & immigration to bring back the footage.

This is in memory of my dear, late friend - and adopted brother - Randy Layson, who died far too soon to travel together to the far side of the globe again.

I'm truly indebted to the amazingly tall and witty, Jimmy Hodson, my seat mate on far too many long flights to remember, with too many great adventures to tell.

Thanks goes to the best professor a promising, older student could ever have had, Dr. Paul Monaco, who expertly taught me the evolution and language of film.

And, finally, to the honorary "El Presidente de Puerto Rico", Sr. Escolastico Mangual, who constantly pestered his son-in-law to write it all down. No more asking me anymore, "how's the book going?"

Introduction

This book began as a short article meant to educate and inform aspiring producers, directors, videographers, crew members, production staff and film students on how to produce and shoot successfully when embarking on any challenging international shoot. Entitled *7 Commando Tactics for Successful Overseas Television & Video Production*, that 2,000 word piece was originally written for *NRB Magazine* back in March 2003. This longer form book, *Commando Tactics for Digital Filmmakers*, is a big leap forward from that short article.

Over the years, many other key principles of the entire digital filmmaking process - from prep to post - began to percolate in my restless mind. So, I started jotting down notes, ideas, concepts, anecdotes, case studies, tips and quotes that might prove helpful to anyone producing or shooting a documentary, video or film. No matter your level of expertise - novice to pro - this practical book is meant to challenge, inform and inspire you. Whether shooting across town, or on the backside of the world, there are certain basic, fundamental principles every production must tackle. In this book I address scores of these project elements, from story to final master.

The visual imagery I employed in my first article years back - and use now - is that of a commando team sent out to accomplish an important mission. It is an analogy still worthy to employ and consider. Because a special ops team, and a television or film crew, share a number of things in common.

First, before a commando group ever storms a beach or lands onto a palace rooftop, they must know their mission. Also, there are many diverse elements critical to their team's success: planning, support, direction, funds, communication, transport, personnel, equipment, logistics, teamwork and flexibility. Just as with a video or documentary shoot, all these elements must work together to accomplish the final goal.

To be clear, *Commando Tactics for Digital Filmmakers* is primarily about single camera, non-fiction production. That style, form and genre are what I know and do best. But elements of storytelling, time management, picking the right camera crew and decision-making work just as productively for an independent film, multi-camera shoot or a dramatic piece too. Over the course of the following chapters, I provide constructive and valuable insights - a field manual of sorts - that include strategies, tips and tactics to make your next digital video or film shoot successful. What I've learned, and now share, is based on hard-earned knowledge and instincts - borne from both success and failure - after extensive travel and assignments for clients and groups across the globe.

Please also realize that what has worked well for me in a foreign country can be just as helpful and useful for you locally too; Solid production principles have no boundaries or locations.

What I really hope you gain from the following pages is a very practical understanding of methods to mount your next shoot more efficiently and effectively. The practical suggestions provided by leading filmmakers, creative talent and colleagues at the end of each chapter are worth gold alone. And please know that the many personal and professional stories I cite along the way are simply meant to provide valuable insight and perspective into the specific topic being explored in that chapter or section.

So, here we go. Prepped and ready? Let's get rolling.

- Craig D. Forrest

CHAPTER 1: STORY

The Story is Your Mission

•

"If you tell a compelling story, they will watch."

- Christiane Amanpour

(CNN Senior Foreign Correspondent)

Amanpour, who is a very well-respected journalist, certainly knows what she's doing. She is perhaps the world's most honored and recognized foreign news correspondent today. Wherever there has been trouble, conflict or news, she has been there almost every time: Bosnia. Afghanistan. Iraq. Israel. Iran. More than anyone in her profession, she knows how to flesh-out a story, land the key interviews - both simple and significant - then bring "the goods" via special delivery live on-the-scene.

Her succinct comment is clear, but valuable: if you tell a compelling story, they (the audience) will watch. Whether the medium for broadcast - or narrowcast - is film, television, documentaries, video or web, people will watch. In film school we learned, as you may have too, that a story is called the *narrative.* It is the telling - the means and methods of communicating your story - that is classified as the *narration.*

The story, and its telling, are equally important. But a good story untold will remain silent until it is discovered and shared. The great telling of a feeble story will ring hollow, no matter the presentation. But if one begins with an interesting, captivating story first, the telling (visually and sonically) will become easier. Combine the two - story and telling - on film, television or video, and you might just have captured lightning in a bottle.

Finding that story, focusing on its various layers, strengths, details and nuances, is the greatest challenge for most any filmmaker, no matter their level of expertise or talent.

Years back, I worked with a novice producer who had virtually no experience in broadcast television, but had unearthed a shocking story involving a growing, alarming trend in child suicides. The producer partnered with someone who provided valuable network connections and possessed considerable talents. Working together, the chilling story of kids killing themselves was eventually produced as an investigative piece by PBS. The fledgling producer, despite lack of experience, won an *Emmy* on her very first project. Nothing wrong with that, and her persistence in exposing such an important societal issue should be - and was - applauded. Story trumped ability. Good.

Get your story right, tell it well, and people will be transformed, moved, inspired, informed, educated or provoked. They might cry, laugh, be enlightened or angry. But they should have a reaction. On the other hand, get your story wrong, and all the editing tricks, fancy camera moves and repeated rewrites in the world probably won't save you.

Your story is your mission. Everything else is just the little details along the way.

Academy award-winning screenwriter, William Goldman, sums up the story process expertly in his great inside-the-industry book on Hollywood filmmaking, *Adventures in The Screen Trade*. In an early chapter, Goldman poses the fundamental question, "What's your story about?" Then, after you've considered your initial answer, the acclaimed writer suggests, that you ask yourself a vital follow-up question, "What's your story *really* about?"

That next question is crucial, because below the surface, down deeper from what might be the obvious themes of your basic story, are more central issues. Those core intangibles often turn out to be the *heart* of your subject. Or might be an important thread, when woven together, that comprises the visible pattern of your story.

For our purposes, this dynamic of what your story is really about permeates most every form of visual media, whether shooting a low-budget feature, a big blockbuster, an independent film, a news segment or a long form documentary.

What's your story? Great. What's it REALLY about?

Stories come in all shapes and sizes. And no two are exactly the same. Yours might be a story of heroism, a biography, sports, tension at the factories, culture, nature, science, wildlife, investigative journalism, political intrigue, a travel piece to a faraway place...or a million other subjects still to be explored. But scratch the surface of the subject you're covering and there is, most likely, a far deeper meaning.

Find out what the narrative is. Focus on your story's center - including the back stories - and you'll rarely go wrong. Tell the story well, and your viewers will follow you.

During that journey, remember this essential element: **Facts go right to the head, but emotions go straight to the heart.** People remember emotions long after the facts or "info bites" have long faded away.

To be clear, the focus of this book is primarily on the process of non-fiction storytelling. (Though there are many helpful tips and tactics offered that can work just as successfully for a fiction piece too.) Truth be told, I have little experience with narrative fiction other than the occasional dramatic vignettes I've directed, plus the actor show reels and improvisational workshops I've shot. My background is in television, video and the documentary form.

In fiction, there most always must be a script written (rough or polished) before physical production commences. That process of long and laborious scriptwriting, initially, is where the narrative is fleshed-out, reworked, and refined - all before the cameras roll (hopefully). A feature script is the blueprint for most everyone in front of (actors) and behind the scenes (producers, director, designers, crew & staff) to work from. More precisely, in fiction it's the director and performers who are telling the story, aided by set designers, wardrobe stylists, directors of photography, and all those special effects people armed with their magical bags of tricks.

By contrast, non-fiction storytelling can launch into production, at least temporarily, without a script. News, for example, is frequently based on events that are happening live: fire, earthquake, a political speech. The list goes on. The story is shaped by real time events, and is told by eyewitnesses, anchors, reporters & crew. Sports is, repeatedly, a live event too. The story unfolds in the game being played, the resolution not known often until the final moment. Sports is all about camera coverage and producing, complimented by informed announcers and commentary.

But most other genres within non-fiction storytelling have some basis in the documentary movement. Non-fiction starts with the spark of an idea, a premise, a story element. The narrative unfolds and develops as other participants are engaged to tell their version of that story. Is there a script? Yes, but sometimes it arrives in the middle or near the end of the production. Interviews shot along-the-way shape the details and steer the story toward new directions. The producers, director and writer choose what they believe are the most important and promising elements. Other footage becomes available, so the story shifts with the strength and details of those visuals. The script reflects those new elements and changes.

As we will see, a *shot list* is a great way to start your production, while the script is still cooking and congealing. Yet, in my experience, you would be surprised how many production crews run across town or the world to shoot an assignment without even a shot list. Many documentary shoots too often begin with fuzzy ideas based on an undefined project, an event or a wish. But, if you don't know the project well or understand how the event might translate into good television, film or video, then you're probably in trouble. And all the editing tricks in the world will rarely save you or your shoot. Winging it rarely gets you anywhere.

You need to grab hold to the horns of your story.

One of the first things I do before ever grabbing gear and heading to the airport is to find out what my story is. If I am shooting for a client with their own story, my query is to ask them: what is absolutely vital to be shot? Describe the crucial "can't miss" elements. Often, the initial answers they provide start to generate a list of four to five key items - a great beginning point. Pursuing your story, doing your due diligence by exploring every potential element, is the sign of a good filmmaker.

Recently, a great television news producer, Don Hewitt, passed away at age 86. He was the legendary executive producer of the iconic, influential TV newsmagazine, *60 Minutes*. The core of what Hewitt firmly believed every meaty interview, exhaustive investigative journalism piece and whimsical feature should possess came down to just four critical words:

Tell Me A Story.

That's it. Tell me a story. All the rest are just details. Hewitt was right.

That's why *60 Minutes* on CBS remains one of my favorite television programs. The series is still successful after more than 40 years because their dedicated team of executives, reporters, producers, crew and editors know how to tell interesting stories well. No tricks, not even a dissolve, fancy graphic or name super. Just great stories about fascinating people, events or news. *60 Minutes*' "raison d'être" (reason for being) is to tell great stories. Ambush interview with a crook. Profiles of courageous people. Interviews with interesting newsmakers. Journeys to a faraway land. It all makes for great, compelling journalism that is story-based at its center.

Telling a good story well is the immovable pillar of non-fiction.

•

SENEGAL, WEST AFRICA

In my upcoming book, *Night Train to Cairo*, I devote a full chapter to my very first trip to Africa back in the mid 80s. My boss, Don, and I were traveling on behalf of a large humanitarian group that provided caring, compassionate relief aid worldwide.

The project Don and I were assigned to shoot was a fundraising video piece featuring a well known inspirational speaker I will call Dr. Tony. He, along with two marketing executives, were to meet up with us in Senegal, West Africa. Our small crew had traveled a few days ahead to the capital city of Dakar to prep gear and acclimate ourselves to the new time zones and intense desert heat.

Even though everyone's intentions were certainly good and noble, there were some road blocks that spelled doom for our shoot from the very beginning.

First, there was no script, plan or even a shot list. The shoot was focused on the abilities of Dr. Tony, and the one week from his crowded schedule he had made available to the client. Our mandate, we were told in prep meetings, was just to get out there on-location in Senegal and "let Tony be Tony." Our host's role was to walk through perceived famine conditions affecting scores of Senegalese villagers, look into our camera lens, and emote. Strike one.

Second, we were heavily dependent on the local African staff to find those tangible stories of malnutrition and starvation farther north along the desolate Senegal River, just across the border from remote, xenophobic Mauritania. The potential stories of devastation didn't really exist, at least not that we had the time or energy to explore in the two days given for physical production. Our band of travelers should have looked harder, dug deeper for story elements, but didn't. That was a key failure for our video project. Strike two.

Finally, specific role definitions hadn't been truly clarified back in the States among the team before we left. On the scene, out in the field weeks later in Africa, Don was asked to direct the talent and villagers, to guide and pull the whole shoot together. Yet, his understanding from the very beginning was that he was only to run camera. As crew, we believed that the executives were there - all excellent fundraisers - to provide the "creative elements" for the project. Strike Three.

Considering all our time traveling, the money spent for airline tickets, hotels, meals, a passenger van, gear, bonding, customs and the little expenses, it all came down to a half day shoot in the dusty, forgotten middle of nowhere. Dr. Tony did a wonderful job off the cuff, and nobody can really be faulted. But the shoot was haphazard, the footage lacked empathy and the dynamics for viewer response, compassion and action were lacking for a successful motivational fundraising piece. The cassette or two of our Senegal road trip sat on an agency shelf for years.

Unfortunately, one can learn as much from failures as one can from successes. Factors on how NOT to do a shoot or story can become permanently etched in one's mind, leading to better principles and tactics later. And I certainly learned a lot from that very first venture to faraway Africa. Even decades later, I can remember clearly what worked, what didn't, and what was learned.

In exotic Senegal, we should have done our homework, asked questions about famine, who was being affected, what their circumstances were right then and there. Were people dying or starving? How badly? What were the root causes? Who could we feature on-camera or talk to? How many days do we have, or realistically need, in the field to make this happen? What's the shooting style? Where's our shot list? How are we going to pull this together? What are the roles of the production team? What do we expect of Dr. Tony? And how can we help him look into a camera, hold a starving child and then ask people watching truly to help?

All of these basic questions should have been hashed out in the States weeks before hitting the airport. Once we landed, a story conference in Senegal would have helped too. But all of these fragmented loose ends were just that: separate threads that we failed to tie together.

Know your story. And get it as right as you possibly can. Style points must never replace or substitute for a good, compelling story that engages, intrigues and grabs your audience.

Your story is the cornerstone on which to build your foundation.

•

STORY BY THE NUMBERS

1. You may encounter many stories along the way. Or discover that there may be various versions. Choose the story you really believe needs telling, that will intrigue a viewing audience by its very nature.

2. Let your *pictures* tell more of the story than the *words* do.

3. Make sure your facts are correct. Check them, verify them. Do your due diligence.

4. When someone is giving you "gold" on-camera during an interview, keep recording. Where their story leads may have far more promise than the story you started with.

•

SHOW AND TELL

Did you ever play "Show and Tell" in Kindergarten or Elementary School? The simple principle actually works very well in formulating non-fiction storytelling too. Before you start your project - or as you're shooting along the way for an "evolving" story - grab a piece of paper (or go to your computer, smart phone or notebook) and break down the page into two halves vertically, top to bottom. On one side (left) list *Show*, the other (right) side *Tell.*

Now, begin listing all the potential visuals you want this specific segment or overall story to capture. List everything you can think of that will *Show* your story: archival footage, b-roll, interviews, re-enactments, still photos, home movies, dramatic setup shots, graphics. Whatever pictorially is appropriate for your theme and story, write it down, list it.

Then on the right side, the *Tell* side, begin listing all the key points that either the written script, narration or the interviewees will be discussing. Write it all down, including important topics, information, facts, trends, story elements, anecdotes and key points the script needs to make.

Film, television and video is a visual medium, so, when you finish, the *Show* side should outweigh the *Tell* side. Conversely, if the script is heavy on facts and information, or your piece seems to be a long string of interviews without supporting cover footage, than the words (Tell) are outweighing the pictures (Show).

Most directors arrange all their best and most memorable sound bites into a proper order based on themes and subjects. That's okay, but many times the program becomes handcuffed by the sound bites, and there is a pressure to fit these clips in because they are great, usable quotes.

Instead, start with your best visuals first. Let your project be influenced by your pictures and footage. Words and great quotes are important and necessary. But, as we've mentioned, people remember the pictures long after the words have faded away.

Pictures are powerful. Use them. Let them drive and influence your segment and story.

SHOW me *most* of the time. TELL me *some* of the time.

•

STORY TACTICS FROM PROS

"Film is a visual medium - the pictures should tell the story. I believe you should be able to understand 60-70% of a foreign film without subtitles."

- Alexander Mackendrick, director

"Emotion gets people to act more than facts."

- Steve Taylor, Digital Spatula

"Stories move people...but it's the truth that changes people."

- Paul Louis Cole, Compass Direct

"Give me the context. When you're shooting an activity have enough video of the surrounding situation to show why the activity is relevant or important.

"Remember the W's...Who, What, Why, When, Where. Be sensitive to the story elements that have the greatest impact, and try to capture them on video."

- Stan Jeter, CBN News

"Be real and tell a good story; the rest will take care of itself!"

- Mark Horvath, Invisiblepeople.tv

"I had a boss at NBC News years ago who always said that whatever we did had to have what he called the 'water cooler' factor.

There had to be something in the story that had an 'oh wow' moment in it that would spark conversation at the coffee machine or water cooler. Some way of looking at an issue, some new fact, something...or else the story was just eating up time."

- Martha Cotton, Plymouth Rock Studios

"Follow your curiosity where it leads you."

- Michael Phillips, Chicago Tribune

"Follow your heart is my only advice."

- Fernando Fonseca, sound designer

"What I tell would-be documentarians is to stop talking about the production process and start shooting instead. Shoot something that's meaningful to you, that shows off your talent and originality, that will let others immerse themselves in your vision. It doesn't have to be a full-length piece; the cost would be prohibitive for most starting filmmakers.

"But while you're waiting around for those all-important first assignments, why not create something that will enhance your chances? I've often encountered shooters, editors and writers who have no experience in the subject matter at hand, but whose work in general captures my eye and, even better, my imagination."

- Burt Kempner, writer-producer

"The proper route to an understanding of the world is an examination of our errors about it."

- Errol Morris, filmmaker (The Thin Blue Line)

"Find and use story arcs. Make sure the documentary takes the viewer on a journey - and make sure there is a beginning, middle and end.

"Make good use of conflict. A great storyteller once told me, some of the most compelling stories tend to have a simple formula - a good guy, a bad guy and a fight!

"Try to let your characters speak for themselves. A documentary is not a newsmagazine piece, so use the omniscient narrator sparingly, if at all."

"B-roll, b-roll, b-roll. Shoot enough video to cover edits in sound bites and to use for transitions and overall aid in visual storytelling. Too many talking heads will end up being a bit of a bore. Always remember to SHOW, DON'T TELL"

- Gregory Branch, producer-journalist

"If you're a newbie - let *Frontline* create and do their version. You should think about how your Point of View is unique, and different and can really make a difference. Then shoot that film. And, whenever possible, shoot compelling 'scenes'. It's the same as fiction filmmaking in that these types of storytelling 'moments' are critical in engaging a viewer, rather than 'expository.'"

- Beverly Peterson, documentary filmmaker

"Sometimes, you'll meet an interesting storyteller. Doesn't matter where, doesn't matter when. Be receptive to a good story and a good storyteller. You just never know - it's all material."

- Alan Lloyd, lighting cameraman

"As a veteran, award-winning editor, I've seen too many independent (read - self-financed and beginning) filmmakers shoot and shoot and shoot and not give much thought to their story beyond the initial idea.

"In response, I've started a workshop, and we really hash out a lot in there that has really been helpful to my students. We think about WHAT do I really want to say or explore with my film?

"We ask HOW do I want to say it?

"What do I want to express? What do I want to say with my film?, and as important...

"Who do I want to say it to?

"Because that 'Who' makes a huge difference is what you're doing, the choices that you're making.

"Sure, you can interview twenty-five people about junk food, or you can follow yourself around while you eat only junk food for a month. The HOW is often the most elegant part of creating a really good doc.

"We also identify the different aspects and wider themes that come up in our story - because really - my favorite documentaries are always Trojan Horses for bigger issues and questions than I realized I was going to get into when I started watching. That is the true gift you give your viewers - so why not start thinking about it before you're done shooting so you can have that material when you start editing?

"My students have all gotten a lot out of going through this process - both in how their final films will end up, but also in terms of saving $'s by shooting what speaks to what they want to say - and how they want to say it."

- Stephanie Hubbard, film & tv editor/producer

"I really liked what Ira Glass has to say about being willing to not accept the first idea and having to discard some pretty good stories to get to something really worthwhile. He also suggests you do a lot of work in the process, but part of refining your taste and getting better is being willing to let go of what isn't working or that good."

- Suzanne LaGrande, media producer

"My advice is this: do not underestimate *Structure* in telling the story. Putting a good deal of thought into the structure of the story you hope to tell, while you're in the midst of planning and shooting, will go a very long way in the editing room. The planned structure can (and sometimes should) change as the process goes on and footage is captured, but when you are facing 50+ hours of footage it will rightfully seem like a near-impossible task without a plan.

"Putting in some time and thought to sketch the skeleton of the story you are telling will mentally equip you to find the right 'flesh' to put on those bones.

"Again, the story will unravel in ways you didn't think of (and your characters and events will help pave this path), but you are the storyteller, and you need to know how you are planning to structure the story in order to keep you on track. It will make your task less daunting, and you'll need to save as much sanity through the long process before you."

- Steve Kearney, Advanced Staging Solutions

"When the product is finished (film) how do you want it to be publicized: TV or film festivals? Being a film festival director and watching a lot of great documentary films I will say this, keep it under 60 minutes. I know sometimes that can be tough, and there's a lot to be said to make the world aware, unfortunately shorter is better."

- Frank Galterio, Kent Film Festival

"1. STORY, STORY, STORY! Doc films absolutely need a story, to be of interest to the general audience.

"2. And a *protagonist* for viewers to relate to. The protagonist can even be the filmmaker.

"3. Locations! Film at interesting, unique locations, and let the audience know where the film takes place.

"4. Do a lot of voice-overs while showing visuals, scenes...try to eliminate all those boring talking heads!

"5. Add in ambient sounds to the sound track.

"6. Keep color, lighting & sound even in all shots, where possible.

"7. Have an Act I, II, III, with a good, memorable climax.

"8. Imagine you're doing a fictional, narrative film.

"9. Pick a subject or theme that is of interest to a wide audience.

"10. Edit and cut relentlessly. Keep it as short as possible."

- Elizabeth English, Moondance Int'l Film Festival

"When I think I'm done with my documentary I ask people who have not seen it to watch it, and after they do I ask them *how long* the piece was. If they tell me a time that was *shorter* than the actual run time, I'm usually OK. If they tell me they think it was *longer* than it really was, I know it needs work."

- Alan Lloyd, lighting cameraman

"Don't be overly attached to your material. I have seen many wonderful documentary films that were flawed because the filmmaker was too attached to scenes, story beats, footage, characters that weren't necessary to the story.

"Production flaws will often be forgiven or overlooked if you tell a great story that has a strong arc and knows when to end. For the novice filmmaker, short films can be great practice for this. It's much harder to write short than long. The lean format forces you to focus on the essentials of your story, and what's not key must drop away."

- Sarah Kass, freelance writer/producer

"It sounds simple, but make sure there's a beginning, a middle and an end. Start every idea, support every idea and finish every idea. Use conflict. Tell your story. Speaking of story - make sure there is one. If you want to make a film about something, make sure you can actually get people to relate to it."

- Jeff Toback, producer @ MLB.com

"People have forgotten how to tell a story. Stories don't have a middle or an end any more. They usually have a beginning that never stops beginning."

- Steven Spielberg, director

CHAPTER 1 REVIEW: STORY

1. Tell me a story.
2. If you tell a compelling story, they will watch.
3. What's your story about? What's it REALLY about?
4. Your story is your mission. Everything else is just the little details along the way.
5. Facts go right to the head, but emotions go straight to the heart.
6. Telling a good story well is the immovable pillar of non-fiction.
7. Your story is the cornerstone on which to build your foundation.
8. SHOW me *most* of the time. TELL me *some* of the time.

CHAPTER 2: PLANNING

Have a Plan

•

"A goal without a plan is just a wish."

- Antoine de Saint Exupery

French writer & aviator

A production team without an organizational plan is destined to be a pretty disorganized group.

Without a plan, you are doomed to failure.

This is true for your project too - from prep to production, all the way through to post. Create a plan. Understand that it can and will change constantly, and anticipate that there will be readjustments and diversions all along the way. No matter the nature of your project, if your shoot requirements are anything beyond just a simple one hour interview with a small camera crew and a microphone, you need to get organized.

Not having a plan is like heading off on a journey without a road map. It is inevitable that you will, eventually, get lost and face trouble around the bend. Count on it. Armed with a road map, you will at least possess an inner sense that you have directions, information and choices. Where you steer, what roads to take, the determining of when, where and how long to stop along the way, is entirely up to you (as driver), and your passengers (who are along for the ride).

For your prep, research, communication, shoots, interviews, footage and editing of your project - you need a plan, some sort of dependable road map and schedule.

Creating a plan will frequently contain lots of variables that depend on the very nature of your medium, shoot and project. A behind-the-scenes look at a blind mountain climbing team attempting to scale Mt. Everest is going to be guided by factors far more diverse than an exposé on insider corruption by rogue stock traders on Wall Street. A profile of the last surviving WWI veteran in Duluth, MN will have little resemblance to a tour video featuring an up-and-coming rock band. These distinct stories and projects represent individual species. Though ideal to be captured on film or video, they require vastly different shooting styles and approaches. But what they *do* share in common is that they all must be organized.

Basically, creating a plan is identifying your genre for shooting, doing your necessary homework, talking to your team, touching base with other important contacts, vendors or resources, then organizing it all together so it makes practical sense. Flying by-the-seat-of-your-pants, or "winging it" as you go, impresses nobody - and wastes valuable time, effort and money.

To be sure, creating a workable plan is equal parts smarts, experience, research, hunches, feedback, information, observation and listening. Much like a military strategist, you hope and plan for the very best, but should also prepare for the occasional disaster too, just to be sure. In my professional case, many of my shoots are overseas. Mix in the unique, exotic blend of faraway locations, foreign cultures (and languages), unpredictable weather and distant time zones, and the challenges multiply. I've often stated that international production is far more difficult then shooting in one's own city or country, because you're continually dealing with foreign environments, unfamiliar people and contacts, plus specific cultural expectations of time, travel and productivity.

In creating a workable plan, first thing out-of-the-box is to get a strong handle on your story elements, at least as much as you might know at the outset. This usually means identifying the various people you need to contact, including managers, crew and talent. Size up the subjects to interview, footage to be shot, plus locations or setups involved. If you must book a studio, then pricing and availability require a phone call, web search, walk through or an e-mail straight away.

When shooting in the field, research as much as possible about the locations (and countries), then formulate logistics based on potential travel, schedules and weather. Find out when key contacts might be available (or not) on-site or those who are traveling as part of the team.

Your project might be a blend of studio and field. So estimate studio time and days on-location for both elements. Break them down, schedule them, anticipate costs, prepare.

Whatever assists you in coordinating this process productively, and effectively, use it. That includes computer scheduling software, weekly calendars, spiral ring notebooks, Excel spreadsheets, mounted cork boards or dry erase boards to break down shoots and timelines. Whatever helps you to stay organized, while allowing you the flexibility to make changes as they occur, go with it.

Get organized.

•

THE PHILIPPINES

Decades later, I can still vividly remember my very first overseas shoot. The assignment was a great learning experience - a short documentary produced for a small humanitarian group I was working for, called OMC, based in California.

OMC's work encompassed projects primarily carried out across the island nation of the Philippines. Programs included on-site work with tribal groups, development collectives, farming education, fishing and boats, and a variety of other very worthy efforts.

Like any small, struggling non-profit agency, our group constantly needed fresh funding and promotions. The idea from our Stateside office was to send a film team and myself to capture OMC's Asian work in the field so as to show potential donors how - with their generous support - our organization could do so much more with extra support.

Looking back, there were some objectives I did right on this project as client/producer, but far too many I failed at too.

Filled with excitement at landing an overseas shoot, I was smart enough to engage a very talented director-cameraman named Lowell. He came with great skills and know-how. Without his sharp abilities, we'd have been lost in the jungle, literally. Since we were shooting on 16mm film, he suggested we should bring along his friend, Dan, to run sound, using a sturdy Nagra recorder. These guys were a really great team - and proved invaluable time and again.

From the USA to the Philippines by air is a very, very long journey. With refueling stops in Anchorage and Seoul, by the time we finally hit Manila we were exhausted physically. Never underestimate how much damage midnight flights, multiple stops and a myriad of time zones can wreak on a person's body, mind and soul. Plus, the heat and humidity of the Tropics can exhaust a person too. It takes some time to acclimate and get your bearings.

One of the true advantages we had was that there was a solid OMC support team in place on-site in the Philippines. These were good, dedicated people I knew rather well, and who had setup each and every step of our proposed shoot in advance. They provided much-needed experience, savvy, logistics, insight, transport and accommodations all along the way.

Over the course of about one week of shooting, we first journeyed south, to Tacloban. There we headed out by open-aired pickup trucks 3 hours drive to Catbalogan, on the remote island of Samar. It was a rural world with incredible beaches, water and greenery, faraway from a busy, modern society. Everywhere we went most Filipinos seemed to ride a bike, with few trucks or cars used. In Catbalogan we captured OMC's work with boats and fishing.

Back to Manila, we shot location office work. Then by truck it was up to the ethereal 2000 year old rice terraces of Banaue, where we filmed our agency's work among the Ifugao tribe, the indigenous peoples of the islands. By covering through film how the Ifugao kept the bones of their dead ancestors wrapped and stored on their back porches, we had met up with *National Geographic* somehow.

We finished up our final interviews in Manila, packed our gear and headed back over the Pacific Ocean to the USA believing we had certainly accomplished our original mission and intent.

Back home, unfortunately, we hit two significant speed bumps.

First, it turned out our small, struggling group didn't have the necessary finishing money to complete the project. Production, yes. But there weren't the extra funds for editing, lab work, sound mixing and completion. Every available penny Stateside was committed to paying the basic bills of running the non-profit office involving salaries, expenses and overhead. There were no extra funds for finishing such a big, special project like a film.

We found ourselves behind the proverbial 8 ball. Without extra monies to complete the film, we couldn't use the new promotional documentary to raise additional funds at banquets and events. Here was an exciting, potential fundraising tool sitting - literally - right on our shelf, stored in film cans, ready for editing.

Second, even though we went into this project with the very best of intentions (most everyone does), we as a group - and I as a producer - really didn't nail down what we truly wanted our film to *show* and *tell*.

Sure, this was meant to be documentary in form, and what was covered professionally by Lowell and Dan expertly illustrated what it was OMC did in the field. *But what was the meaning of it all?* By that I am suggesting that we just didn't have enough inspiring moments - either in interviews or footage - that would really cause our viewers to get excited about OMC's work in Asia.

Without some memorable moments, our little documentary film was going to fall flat.

Explanation is fine, but it's imagination that sparks the fire. Remember our goal: raise money and awareness. We needed more "ah ha" moments. More compelling material was needed to take the viewer from *passive observer* to *interested participant.*

Our last grasp at funding was my showing some of the raw footage to one of our most important, major donors at his home. He was a very wealthy person who could easily have written one check to complete our project. But, as we showed the rolls of film to him, it was just cover footage of our work in the Philippines, the B-roll. Boats, water buffaloes, tribal people, office workers. No interviews or explanation or script.

From what we were projecting onto his home screen that night, he didn't see much potential. Neither did I. The film languished, never to be completed.

(Word to the wise: be careful - *never* if you can - to show raw, unedited footage to "big shots". Unless they can fathom how what they are seeing will turn into something finished and magical - don't do it. It's a recipe for disaster. Show them footage that is as close to completed as possible, requiring very little explanation.)

As I look back at that first, feeble attempt of mine at a documentary, I come away with some well-earned observations.

Figure out your plan well *before* you head to the airport.

Get some real bones to your story upfront. Know what you want to *show* and *tell* - and how it fits the purpose of your project.

Make sure there is *clear communication* all along the way. That includes *role definitions*.

In my case, I really thought I knew what I was doing, having briefly worked for a television network before that project. In my naïveté, I exuded a bit of cockiness that didn't sit well with the crew at times. And rightly so. They didn't listen to me. Because I hadn't earned their trust and respect. Their perspective was that they were doing our group a favor by shooting this extremely low budget project for minimal compensation; They were mostly along for a merry adventure to the Philippines.

In retrospect, with such little experience in the film production and the documentary form, the best course would have been for me to sit-down with Lowell and Dan at the very beginning and let them know just how little experience I had - and that I really needed their help. That I'd never done a shoot or project like this one before. And that I was open to *anything* I could learn from them on this project. Suggestions. Tips. Tactics. Ideas.

There are times to be confident and bold...but other times where it's best simply to be humble and quiet.

More than 80 trips and nearly 200 assignments later, I am no longer that young greenhorn who boarded a Korean Airlines jet those many years ago with stacks of luggage and a film crew of three.

Now I see a story as it takes shape, know better how it can be used in the final edit, and how it should play on the screen. Lessons learned.

They say a journey of a thousand miles begins with just one step.

The Philippines was my first step.

•

PLAN DETAILS

SCHEDULE: How many locations? Days in the field? How many hours in a studio or on-set? Start shaping the amount of time expected for production as soon as possible. Shooting days tremendously affect one's budget (and the project timeline), for they add up and multiply, going straight to the bottom line. Know that hardly any two shoots are the same. Four days in South Africa are different than three days in a New York studio.

A two day shoot on the streets of Los Angeles or Seattle, in comparison with a project shot and edited in a factory in San Antonio, are apples versus pineapples. If you are shooting in eight locations across your country with five travels days for thirteen days combined of production - out and back - with a four person crew, a producer and a director, then factor all these logistics, variables and requirements into your schedule.

One effective plan is to start thinking from the back to the front.

- When is the delivery or show date?
- When does the project need to be finished and duplicated?
- How many days in post-production will be necessary (including sound mix and music)?
- How many days for production are needed or anticipated?
- When do we start to shoot?

- What's the earliest or latest time to start pre-production?
- What does this all add up to?
- Where are we at RIGHT NOW date wise???

PRE-PRODUCTION: Most projects are in a hurry due to last minute, rushed decisions. So the client, agency or production company prep process gets squeezed from an adequate amount of pre-production to a squeezed amount, sort of like a trash compactor doing its evil chore. Time and again, I've seen projects that slashed prep in an attempt to save money, or due to poor, inadequate planning. Then staff and crew jump into production far too soon, resulting in far greater amounts of the budget being spent in working *faster* rather than *smarter*.

Leave lots of room for prep if at all possible, as prep saves far more money to the project budget than it usually wastes.

CREW: How many people do you need? What is the size of the staff and crew? What are their roles? What's the budget? Also consider hiring a DP or gaffer to help light, plus renting a lighting kit or small grip truck. Professionals who light creatively add tremendous aesthetic value to the shoot's look. Your money continually ends up on the screen.

It's the same for audio. My experience is that sound personnel will run the microphone lines correctly the first time, and uncover a pesky audio problem early, notifying the producer and director to potential troubles. You can have the best lit setup in the world, but if your audio is scratchy, or the wireless mic is picking up the airport control tower, you're in deep trouble. *Poor audio defeats great lighting every time.*

TRAVEL: Research airline schedules, possible hotels/motels, transport, local costs. Sometimes, for smaller shoots, I've rented drivable motor homes to serve as part makeup trailer, crew quarters and production HQ. The benefit is that the vehicle can move easily to your next setup, has its own bathrooms and can be used for creative meetings. Plus, when it's time for the midday lunch, food, snacks and drinks can be stored in the little kitchen.

GEAR: If your group owns its own digital equipment, great. Often, I rent gear because formats and equipment specs change frequently, so I will hire talented, experienced camera, sound and technical personnel who are owner-operators offering their own gear packages as well. The benefit is that they know their equipment intimately, take great pride in caring for their gear, and will sometimes give the production company a break on the rental price. Gear and crew come as a negotiated package. They also bring their equipment - cases of it sometimes - with them to the shoot, thus saving pickup costs and delivery time.

OUTSIDE SERVICES: Consider that if you are engaging in a more complicated shoot that requires:

- Studio and/or various separate locations
- Multiple cameras
- Trailers
- Lighting or grip trucks
- Generators
- Craft services (food) and/or meal catering
- Props or wardrobe
- Sets
- Security

...then you are now venturing into a bigger plan or organization than just a one camera, three person sit-down interview with some b-roll scheduled. Anything beyond a camera and a half day will require a lot more details. Roll up your sleeves: you've got some work to do - in prep, crew, facilities, ordering supplies, gear, paying the bills and tying up all loose ends afterwards.

Truth be told, you may need some help. Production Assistants - what I call *worker bees* - are there to help you, and they are worth the added extra costs to tackle individual parts of your plan. This might include scheduling, delivery, running errands, picking up people at the airport, buying sandwiches and bottled water. Extra hands will help your team "divide and conquer."

EDITING: Using *Final Cut Pro* on your laptop to cut your project? Going to a boutique editing company featuring *Avid*? Need an assistant editor, loggers and someone to "sweeten" sound? Going to a high end post house to finalize and deliver? How many days and weeks do you anticipate the entire editing process to take?

Post-production is a major factor for finishing your project, large or small. Sometimes more budget money is spent on post than the production itself depending on the nature of the story and shoot. Having a reasonable idea at the very start of how much time you might need to complete your show, film or segment will help you tremendously in the overall plan.

And, yes, things always change. *Bank on it.*

That award-winning star editor who wasn't originally available now has an open schedule. Negotiate their rates, check with the producer or director, book them. Adjust the plan.

Your post-production supervisor wants a rough cut, first or fine cut finished sooner than you anticipated. Adjust the plan.

The director has located a couple of new, important interviews to shoot "green screen" that need to be added as soon as possible to the nearly finished edit. Check the budget, call your crew, re-work the editing timeline. Adjust the plan.

My best advice is to give yourself more time - if at all possible - in post-production than you think might be necessary. Editing is a fun, creative part of the process, and remains a wonderful laboratory to experiment, make changes and fine tune. You'll want to try different versions of your project, add graphics, efx, create title sequences, lay down the music tracks.

Allow enough time for the editing process. Your project will be far better for it.

•

SCRIPT OR SHOT LIST?

In non-fiction, the story often unfolds little by little, in layers, like building a sandwich. The script may be in flux, continually written and rewritten, created "in pencil" as you go, using the proverbial "eraser" to make changes here and there. So it's perfectly okay to start with a SHOT LIST. Many times the story elements are still jelling and coming together as new interviews are being recorded, while b-roll (including footage, pictures and graphics) is also added to the project. Starting with a shot list for the individual segments of your production is a reasonable plan for shooting sequences as they are researched, scheduled and recorded.

PREP: Before booking an interview or shoot, research as much of the story over the phone, in-person or via e-mail with the subjects to be interviewed (or main contacts) as possible. Ask questions, including identifying key visuals to support the story. Write down a tentative shot list to work from that goes beyond just the interview or setup itself. Even if your project is still a "work in progress," a shot list will help as you attempt to get a handle on your shoot and story.

If you're traveling on-assignment overseas or cross-country, or even doing just a straight forward shoot across town, talk to the producer, production manager or client and ask them what their expectations are for the shoot. What do they want covered? Who's being interviewed? What's the schedule? How much time do they expect is needed? What's the setup? Is this indoors or outdoors? Gathering this information first will help you prepare and get organized.

PYRAMID SHOT LIST: Over the years in working with scores of clients, groups and organizations, I've developed a little tactic that saves everyone - including the crew and staff - a lot of time, trouble and frustration. I call it the *Pyramid Shot List.* No matter if you're working with someone for the very first time or the twenty-fifth, I ask the person or group to send a detailed list of possible topics and supporting visuals (b-roll or cutaways) they'd like us to shoot. Basically, through teamwork and communication, we're creating a *tentative* ("in pencil") shot list.

From that list, they are asked to identify THE MOST IMPORTANT ELEMENTS at the top. Then they are to rank or categorize other shots and subjects of *lesser* importance further down the list, item by item, until we arrive at the *very least important* objectives (near the bottom). This is where the *Pyramid Shot List* becomes useful: Important at the very *top*, least important down at the *bottom.*

By asking a producer or client to help create a shot list, I am drawing information and goals from them that assist the shoot. Instead of ideas stuck in their brain - that perhaps only *they* know - we're getting those ideas spelled out on a common, workable list, which becomes part of the production plan. In addition, the *Pyramid Shot List* helps to cut down on any possible miscommunication about who and what we're shooting, while also rank ordering the process.

Armed with this shot list - created with the producer or client by phone, web or in-person - I'll know better what's important to the project on that day's shoot. Remaining flexible, our team will try as hard as possible to shoot everything on the list, top to bottom. (And I will ask what the significance and importance of the items down the list are too.) But, for sure, the crucial "can't miss" elements on top are handled first. (If I am the director or producing the shoot, I will create the shot list myself, for this run list keeps me on track, helping me to focus on what's really important - or not.)

Overall, the *Pyramid Shot List* defines intentions and expectations for most any shoot. Sizing up the shot list also benefits the production in regards to scheduling and budgeting time. If the shot list is too long and detailed, or is filled with a long list of "must have" objectives, I will need far more time than we had originally planned. Either we pair down the list, or add more shoot time. Something has to budge, which is better to know BEFORE the shoot.

Your shot list - in non-fiction storytelling - becomes part of the plan. The list further assists the story process by helping to form the eventual script - by identifying subjects, themes and visuals that are more critical than others.

•

CAMEROON, CENTRAL AFRICA

In the late 90s I got a phone call on the very same day I was heading to Central Africa to cover a week long speaking event. A good group, *International Aid*, had learned I was traveling to the very same remote city in upcountry Cameroon where they had built a small eye clinic. My evenings for the speaking event were already booked, but my days were basically free to shoot projects and footage locally, if asked.

The humanitarian group engaged my services verbally by phone, and we agreed on two days of shooting while I'd be in Cameroon. Before leaving for the airport to travel through Europe to Africa during the next couple days, I asked this new client to create a shot list detailing the most important visuals, topics and objectives they wanted me to cover. There wasn't enough time in a quick phone conversation on departure day to create such a list in advance, for I was literally packing my bags and heading overseas. My contact was to fax that list to their clinic in Maroua, Cameroon ahead of my arrival. From their list, I'd handle the production for them. Put the "must have" shots at the top, less important "if you have extra time" items at the bottom – the *Pyramid Shot List.*

Once I hit the ground in Cameroon, people from the *Binder Eye-Care Hospital* - a really great group doing wonderful, compassionate work - drove out and picked me up on the first day at my local hotel. The requested shot list from the sponsoring group in Michigan still hadn't arrived in Cameroon yet. And because of the six hour time difference between *International Aid* and the Maroua hospital, I rolled up my sleeves and decided to create my own list to get started.

Sitting down over coffee at the clinic, I started asking the doctors and operational leaders what the most important areas of eye care were to them:

- What does your clinic do best?
- What is your motivation for compassion?
- What types of patients do you assist?
- What are the typical ages of those being helped?

- What types of surgeries do you perform the most?
- What's the worst you encounter? The easiest?
- What difference does surgery make for the people you assist?
- Why do doctors donate their vacation time to help you by performing surgeries?

Their great, dedicated team of doctors, nurses, managers and staff began describing their work among the Cameroonians in this dry, remote region. They explained that the vast majority of patients were terribly poor and could not afford such surgeries. Most common treatments were simple, but necessary, like removing cataracts. I toured their facility, asked follow-up questions, and surveyed what their story (and mission statement) was all about.

I began to think of visuals to shoot, and topics that needed covering by interview, to *show* and *tell* this motivational story effectively in a short video. Creating a shot list, I began writing down footage and subjects, starting with the most important objectives down to the very least.

From that list, I interviewed doctors on-camera about their reasons for volunteering. Captured footage of basic eye operations in the surgery rooms. Got master shots and close-ups of the sick and afflicted in the waiting room. Outside shots of people traveling by foot or bicycle to the clinic. Recorded close-ups and master shots of those being assisted during their initial checkups with nurses. Shot emotional interviews with actual patients, before and after surgeries, plus their family members. We asked key medical and operational staff to speak about the work and success of this special clinic. Gathered footage of signage and the grounds, so that facts and narration could be added later. As much as possible, we recorded patient care everywhere it was happening, including clinic treatment with lots of "hands on" medical assistance performed.

When it was early in the morning - best light of the day and cooler in temperature - we captured the various outdoor shots and interviews. When the heat kicked up, and the sun got brighter at midday, we moved indoors for interior footage, and shot some interviews in the shade. What we could not capture that first day, we saved for the second - balancing out the shoot overall. Throughout our shooting days, I checked off possible interviews, interesting topics, important shots, angles, surgeries, people, facilities and procedures we'd recorded.

Finally, the client's shot list arrived by fax in the very last hour during the second shoot day. It arrived after 99% of our time had been already used for production using my own list created that very first morning. Thankfully, we had - through conversation, questions, observation and instinct - already shot virtually every single item on the client's final shot list. All we were missing were a few requested b-roll shots showing the living quarters on-site, meant to illustrate for doctors where they would stay when traveling to volunteer at the clinic. We shot some cover footage, then we were done. Every item on our shot list was checked off.

No script? Changing/evolving script? Create a Pyramid Shot List.

•

PLANNING TACTICS FROM PROS

"In broadcasting, I learned the hard way how prepared you need to be to be spontaneous."

- Walter Cronkite, CBS News anchor

"Know your story and follow a shot list. Think through the elements you need to have to tell the story, and keep your editor happy, making sure you get every shot you need. This also means organizing your on-location work so everything is covered in the time available. When time is limited, go for the main shots first, then take care of the rest. This is especially important if bad weather or other interruptions threaten your shoot."

- Stan Jeter, CBN News

"Know every piece of equipment before you drive out to that remote spot with no cell reception or AC power.

"Preview the production from the end backward - from the delivered master back to the camera tape or SD card. If you can see the production clearly backwards, you will see what will be needed and when."

- Dustin Ebsen, Beantown Productions

"If you know what you want before you begin the shoot, you'll know when you get it. Thorough pre-production makes for an efficient, creative shoot. That allows for time to capture other shots of opportunity.

"Never say it will be an easy shoot. I don't believe in jinxes, but when people (crew, talent, clients) hear 'easy', their attention to detail drops slightly, and the shoot always takes longer. Keep everyone focused on productivity and quality. If it goes quickly, and well, celebrate with them!"

- Don Hancock, Performance Communications

"Try to plan ahead for locations and times to charge batteries."

- Steve Taylor, Digital Spatula

"Before you begin to shoot, plan your elements."

- Gregory Branch, producer-journalist

"Factor in things like the potential for rain on outdoor shoots (have a Plan B), and other possible - and uncontrollable - delays."

- Alan Lloyd, lighting cameraman

"A successful shoot really requires a number of things:

"1. A clear idea of what HAS to be shot.

"2. Coordination with ground staff and contacts.

"3. Great planning.

"4. Flexibility.

"5. Crew to be placed in environments that allow them to rest and maximize their time in the communities."

- Jim Rawn, Year 64 Media

"Just Do It. Newcomers often face a lot of self-censorship. There is no lesson that beats picking up a camera and starting to shoot, then finding a way to edit your material and screening it in front of anyone willing to watch. Along the way, they will discover what works & doesn't work for them after they've produced their first project, then their second, etc.

"One mentor also advised me, 'Think about the shots that worked and what you did to get them' after reviewing some material for a project.' I still consider that advice very valuable."

- Angelike Contis, reporter/documentary-maker

"New filmmakers often jump into production before they've done all of the necessary planning and final script writing. This can be very hazardous, a waste of money and time. Make sure you Plan, Write, Research and do a little more Planning! The outcome will be outstanding and may just find you a little dinero along the way!"

- Michelle Haynes Alvarado, Wahoo Films

"Give some quality time on planning. It shows in the final product. Attention to details is too important. The message should let the audience think for days. The message should be linked well with the whole movie. The lighting, the emotions, the music, camera movements all should be in alignment.

"Observe nature, people, environment, you can get a lot of things you need. Believe in your idea, do not change your track due to suggestions."

- Shibu Abraham, filmmaker

"Beware of tunnel vision during research; there might be another plausible explanation that doesn't fit your train of thoughts.

"Check, check and double check, check that again and check that!

"At the end of the interview, keep the camera rolling and aimed. You'll be surprised how informal people really sound giving additional information."

- Wim Maatman, owner, Mediagroep Gelderland BV

CHAPTER 2 REVIEW: PLANNING

1. A goal without a plan is just a wish.
2. Without a plan, you are doomed to failure.
3. Get organized.
4. Get a handle on your story elements, as much as you might know at the start.
5. One effective plan is to start thinking from the back to the front.
6. Prep saves far more money to the project budget than it usually wastes.
7. No script? Changing/evolving script? Create a Pyramid Shot List.
8. Allow enough time for the editing process. Your project will be far better for it.
9. Things always change. Bank on it.
10. Explanation is fine, but it's imagination that sparks the fire.

CHAPTER 3: INTERVIEWING

Art of the Interview

•

"The best questions often come
from the previous answer."
- *Ted Koppel*
(ABC Network's Nightline)

I've always liked the television program *Nightline*, remembering its roots as a late night news show detailing the status of the American Embassy staff held hostage by protesting Iranian students in the late 1970s. Its original title was *America Held Hostage.*

Koppel, the superb host for twenty-five years, is one of the best interviewers around, always asking solid, penetrating questions. He does his journalistic homework, listens, anticipates, probes, follows up, stands his ground. Sometimes the cross talk results in a three ring circus atmosphere, but Koppel has always been a consummate pro. And the quality (and quantity) of his interviews with the famous - and infamous - ranks the journalist within the same pantheon of most any serious news host you could ever find in the history of television broadcasting.

His succinct statement is one of the most important communications dynamics in how one conducts an interview - whether you are talking to a head of state, a convicted murderer, a star athlete or the night security guard that locks the front doors at the car plant that just got robbed.

After your thorough preparation, asking good, intelligent interview questions comes down to *listening* - paying attention, being in the moment, anticipating, following-up on a dangling thread of response.

If you are only thinking of your next question, then you are failing as a filmmaker, interviewer and communicator.

If the list of questions on your clipboard has become more important than the person speaking right in front of you, then you, and your project, are in serious trouble.

To be fair, you may get lucky. The person you're speaking with might provide such great answers, and prove such a memorable guest, that no matter *what* you ask them, it won't really matter. Because their wit, personality, observations or keen knowledge will make you - along with the story and interview - shine. Then again, perhaps not.

Let's lay down some basics for a moment.

In the overall context of recording stories there remain just a few cinematic elements that provide actual content and information. In the non-fiction form, content derives most often from two primary sources: First, *narration,* which can include an off-screen announcer or an on-screen host (or hostess) reading a script, cue card or teleprompter. The other key component prominently featured is the *on-camera interview.* (Another element meant to augment both narration and interview is *on-screen graphics.*)

Interviews, consistently, are the staple - the bread and butter - of most any non-fiction TV segment, film, video, dvd or documentary.

So, how you engage the person(s) interviewed is vital to the success of your project, segment or story. And, it should go without saying, you *must* do your research, which includes subject, topic and location. Interviews, which come in various shapes and sizes that we will discuss in this chapter, are crucial. Let's say it again: CRUCIAL.

Working from both the technical or creative sidelines, it continues to amaze me how many people will tell you most anything if you listen *closely.*

The *follow-up questions* - the one's not on your original list - are key. Because those new paths of exploration will often steer the discussion into new, unintended directions. Most of the time - but not always - these unexpected, surprising topics will add layers, nuance and details to the story you are exploring, shooting and presenting.

Yes, as Koppel surmised, the best questions usually come from the previous answer, because someone has just said something worth following-up on. That's when good interviews truly begin. For most interviews are organic; they develop through a process of give and take, the development of the relationship between the subject being questioned, and you, the interviewer.

So, listen and follow-up. But, then again, don't be afraid to improvise when necessary. It is *your role* as a filmmaker to steer the ship. Do navigate well, but try not to fall off the edge of the world while at the helm.

•

CALIFORNIA

Years back, I was doing an investigative journalism shoot at the *California Youth Authority* in Whittier, CA. It was for a good, but forgotten tv series called *Case Closed*, then playing on *USA Network*.

My job was to run sound for the interviews, connecting a single lapel microphone straight to the camera while also watching the record levels. Throughout the production day the law enforcement officers brought a series of young male rapists to a side building where our crew would interview these prisoners on-camera. Many of these inmates were from the barrios of Southern California, most having grown up in gangs. These guys were a very tough group, with shaved heads, plenty of tattoos and attitude.

Starting out, the field producer asked some basic questions about each criminal's past convictions, including circumstances of abuse and rape. All standard, by-the-numbers interviewing. This straightforward style of enquiry went on for a whole morning, our spending about 20-30 minutes on-camera with each inmate. To be fair, nothing was really working, no great material was forthcoming.

During an especially long interview break, the field producer asked James (cameraman) and I (sound) if there were any other questions *we* thought might be good to ask. After thinking about it for a moment or two I offered just one simple suggestion:

"Ask these guys what they think of women. What's their viewpoint on females?"

The next male rapist came in, and the field producer went about asking the same set of questions he'd used before, then he switched and asked the new question: "What do you think of women?"

The change in response was instantaneous. You could have felt a shiver go down your spin, because the emotional electricity in the room changed dramatically just with that simple, piercing question the field producer now asked.

The inmate started spewing out words laced with hatred, disdain and contempt for his past girlfriends and other women he knew. From his viewpoint, women were contemptible "bleeps" who were manipulative and brazen. To him, they *deserved* what they got.

When asked about the woman he had been convicted of raping, his comments were so vile and venomous that I cannot print them in this book. Yet, by asking a new, crucial question it was as if the viewer was now peering into a social and sexual sewer filled with degradation, abuse and misogyny. Powerful, and certainly not pretty.

Hate to admit it, but this complete change of direction made for great TV. Of course, the coarse language would have to be bleeped where necessary, but by digging just a little deeper, changing course from facts to emotions, the field producer was gathering solid sound bites and content. Yes, the interview material on-camera was offensive, but, alas, perfect for a crime show.

The inmate's comments revealed a dirty window into the soul of a violent rapist.

Asking the criminal his view of women was the right question to ask. The field producer's willingness to think beyond the clipboard and standard set of questions resulted in shocking, compelling interview material.

•

KEY QUESTIONS

I've found over time that one of the keys to success in conducting interviews is to rarely ask "Yes" or "No" questions - for they often provide very short answers that lead, basically, nowhere.

Extremely short answers can often prove to be an embarrassing disaster on-camera, for they provide little depth and promote an awkwardness. As interviewer, you want to both engage and draw out your subject to express their opinions and tell their story.

So, as a director/interviewer, I repeatedly ask my subjects questions that begin with *Tell, Describe, Explain* and *Talk.*

For example:

- **Tell** me about your life growing up here in Tulsa.
- **Describe** was that was like as a kid.
- **Explain** to me how times were very different back then.
- When we talked earlier you mentioned that you had a terrible car accident that left you paralyzed in one leg at age eleven. **Talk** to us about the circumstances of that tragedy.

If you begin with a direct question like, "did you have a car accident as a kid?", the answer might be adequate, but probably much shorter than "describe for us how the car accident happened."

Such a question might also lead to long, rambling, out-of-control answers that lead nowhere and are, worse yet, difficult to edit.

The late Johnny Carson, legendary host of America's *The Tonight Show* (NBC) for 30+ years, used to have a great setup question when interviewing his guests. Carson would often ask a question in disguise: "...someone told me that..." Then he would ADD a subject matter.

"Someone told me that...you just came back from a great concert tour to Eastern Europe."

"Someone told me that you really love to go big game hunting in Africa."

"Someone told me that there is a new, special person in your life."

First, that "someone" was a researcher on Carson's staff who had pre-interviewed the guest and had created a question list for the host.

Second, and more critical to interviewing, the "someone told me" question was an easy way for Carson to "draw out" the subject so they would talk - comfortably - about something important to them.

Use Tell, Describe, Explain, Talk...and, even perhaps, "someone told me..."

•

THE SIT-DOWN INTERVIEW

Sit two people on chairs in a well-lit setting, provide a great subject, roll tape (or record to memory) and you have the beginnings of a story, show or segment.

But to tackle a successful sit-down interview you need adequate time. Because to make it work, the lights, sound, chair positions and little knickknacks in the background (tables, lamps, books in the bookcase, pictures of the family) all have to turn into a visual painting.

A colleague of mine, cameraman Sergio Montoya, used to ask the producer or director just before setting up an interview, **"do you want this FAST or GOOD?"**

Montoya is right; you rarely, if ever, have time for both.

Fast means a quick setup, lights up (or use of available light), people mic'd, chairs set, adjust, reframe, push record.

Good means taking a *minimum of 30-60 minutes* to make sure lighting is proper, chairs set to their best advantage, microphones ready and that all the little details in the camera frame are placed appropriately (not to compete, but to compliment). Try to think of the background details as *supporting cast*; the person being interviewed should be considered the *feature player* of the segment and shot.

For time reasons, please keep in mind that in choosing a sit-down interview that it will also take some time to strike the setup, lights usually being put away last due to their hot temperature. That means bags packed, cables wrapped, gear packed and the need to put all the interior elements back to their original places.

Rule for Sit-Down Interviews: always leave a room as good - or better - than you found it. You're a guest, usually, in someone else's place (office, home, workspace, house of worship). Put everything back so it looks as if you've never even been there with your team.

Whether you use one, two or three cameras to cover the sit-down shoot is up to a number of factors: budget, shooting style, size of room, importance of subject, number of crew available, creative vision and whether the interviewer will be seen on camera, etc.

But, having an extra camera - to get close-ups, angles or a master shot - will bring applause from your editor when the interview is cut together. The extra camera(s) provides coverage to liven up the segment with energy between camera angles.

If you are using multiple cameras, make sure the team has a defined plan as to who covers what and when. One camera might be shooting a close-up, the other a master shot simultaneously. Whatever the angles and scheme, make sure *before* the interview starts that everyone is on the same wave length. If the scheme isn't working during the interview, stop record, adjust, talk, then move on.

One of the pitfalls of most any interview - including the sit-down - include distractions. They may come in the form of a telephone ringing in the room, a person walking in unannounced, air conditioner noise (called "white noise") or a myriad of other little, pesky things that jeopardize both the flow of the interview, plus the images and sounds recorded.

Having as much control over the physical room is crucial to the interview's success, whether in front of or behind the camera.

Always take a moment to record ambient (natural sound) sometime during the shoot. I like to have everyone stay quiet for a moment (15-30 seconds) while framing a close-up shot of the lapel microphone or boom pole. This way the editor or sound mixer can easily identify the location of "natural sound" by going straight to the microphone shot.

Also consider shooting cover shots (master shots) of the interview before, during or after the actual Q&A sequence. Sometimes this can be done by a second camera, including over-the-shoulder shots, singles, two shots, reversals, back of the room and behind-the-scenes.

Together, these angles and cover shots provide the filmmaker with other possibilities to introduce *voice-over* into the final version, while also establishing the subject just before their answers. Cover shots also allow the cutting together of two different sound bites for editing reasons, with the ability to cover that edit with an over-the-shoulder reaction or a wide shot.

If time allows, make sure to take a few moments to shoot footage of the subject in their natural environment, i.e., working at their desk, talking to colleagues, examining a patient or walking into their building. Setup shots - your subject doing something that matches the story and/or their role - further define the story and segment.

•

SPINELLI LENS

Just before the interview is to start - in the informal conversation between subject and interviewer - people often begin offering excellent responses that prove great for on-camera. Yet the camera is not in record yet, because no one has asked to start.

One of the quiet ways to get rolling includes a trick I learned from a late, great cameraman friend. Randy Layson had a secret signal with his field producer on Fox Network's *A Current Affair* as to "when" to push the record button before an interview. If the subject was saying great things desired for on-camera, the producer would quietly turn and ask, "Randy, did you bring the Spinelli Lens?"

Randy would invariably say, "Sure, I have it right here." (There is no such thing as a Spinelli Lens.) This was the producer's quiet signal to start record without the person knowing. Randy would smoothly hit the red button, and the interview was on.

Sometimes it would be five minutes into the shoot before the subject realized they'd even started. By then, they'd already given a great comment or two. Smart, because the more natural and unrehearsed people are, the better and less nervous they usually appear on-camera. Saying "ROLL TAPE" or "LET'S START" often *freezes* people in front of the camera, making them nervous. Recording without their knowing it captures people in a much more natural state.

So, do you have the *Spinelli Lens* with you?

•

THE WALKING INTERVIEW

By their very nature, walking interviews are conducted on the move. Whether on the street, along a river or through a factory, it's primarily a focus on interviewer and subject. Maybe you stop along the way, point out something or somewhere interesting, for example, where the person went to school, or shot the victim, or nearly got hit by a bus.

But you move constantly.

In my experience, a couple of technical and staging principles need to be decided to make this type of interview truly successful.

First, either wireless microphones or a "shotgun" mic with fish pole (and sound man) are absolute necessities to capture sound properly. If you are using the on-board camera mic, buy the best you can afford and stay close to the subjects. But unless it's a quiet environment, expect street noise and raw audio to be recorded too, making it difficult in the edit suite, sound mixing bay or on your laptop. That's when a unidirectional wireless or shotgun microphone will save your sound mix.

Second, the moving interview is very physical, hard work for the cameraperson, who must often walk backwards to capture the scene. Make sure, especially if there is uneven terrain or pavement, that a camera assistant or grip is guiding him/her and bracing them to save from a potential fall or slip.

Third, lighting can wreak havoc as the interview moves between light and shade outdoors or through artificial light indoors. Make sure your camera iris is set properly to cover both sunlight and shade. Having some form of portable light - either carried, pointed or on-board the camera - helps too in dark setups. Many times a reflector or white poster board can also help.

Fourth, try not to go more than 20-30 minutes of walking and talking, especially if shooting outside in hot, cold or wet weather conditions. Walking interviews are very exhausting. Keep them short whenever possible.

Finally, make sure to get various long shots and reactions for visual coverage. If you need to trim down the interview for length, timing and content - or cover mistakes and edits - long shots and different angles help immensely.

Having a second camera pays major dividends when editing too.

•

THE GROUP INTERVIEW

I have done interviews with eight people before: two asking questions and six subjects. It's very difficult. You need a mic for every person (or a boom), a multi-channel sound mixer, ample lighting (if indoors), and a plan. It's a lot like directing traffic, for if someone speaks spontaneously one of your cameras has to grab their comments as soon as possible. Knowing *who* is going to speak and *when* is crucial.

Unless it's a live interview, be willing to pause between comments, decide who will speak next, frame a shot on that person, then record.

To cover a group interview really requires, at the minimum, two cameras. One camera is meant to frame a master shot, and the other to get close-ups and two shots (two people in frame). A third camera, if practical, is ideal for framing the interviewer asking their questions and for turning to get side angles, reverse angles and reaction shots (very important).

Group interviews are difficult. So bring two-three cameras, lots of lights + sound, a full crew, monitors and develop a plan to cover everyone. Prepare to take your time, because group interviews rarely go quickly due to setup, coverage and number of people involved - on both sides of the camera.

•

THE AMBUSH INTERVIEW

These are on-the-fly and often *confrontational.* Why? Because you are sticking a camera and microphone into a person's face at a time and place when they don't expect it. They might comply, or they might get agitated. Prepare for the worst, like a door slammed, a camera shoved, being escorted off the property by security personnel or having profanity shouted at you.

To start, make absolutely sure that your sound and camera are properly prepared. Don't wing it, because you might only get one chance. Hit *record* long before you walk into the person's office, knock on their front door or catch them coming out the back door.

Next, do not stop recording until well after the person is finished speaking, or the segment is recognizably over with. Better to stop recording too late, than hit the red button too early. Because you don't know what the person will say, or when they will stop speaking.

Finally, be prepared for a reaction, which can come in many forms, including violence, aggression, shouting, humbleness, evasion, silence or contrition. Realize you are shooting an ambush interview for a reason: you couldn't get the person to sit-down for a formal interview.

Remember, just keep rolling until the director or producer has told you to stop.

•

THE ON-LOCATION STAND UP INTERVIEW

Of all the types of interviews I've done, I have the most experience with the single person, on-location setup, having shot hundreds of stand ups. Placing people in cool places like in Moscow's Red Square, outside the domed churches of the Ukraine, along Victoria Falls in Zimbabwe or perched on the banks of the Ganges is artistically and professionally fulfilling. Such landmarks - and many others - lend atmosphere and presence to the interview itself.

That's why to my mind - creatively, visually, aesthetically - nothing tops an interesting person positioned in a visually dynamic location speaking on a subject that is equally informative and compelling. It's all about a wonderful conversation in a great place.

To be truly successful, there are just a few key ingredients required. But they are crucial; miss one and it's like a shaky three legged stool - it all falls down.

LOCATION: Find a standup spot for the interview that fits the story you are telling. It should be appropriate to both the subject and questions. In fact, location is the *supporting cast* to whatever the theme of your segment is and person being interviewed. *Placement is critical.*

SOUND: Make sure you have good audio, either by hard-wired lavaliere, shotgun mic, wireless or, lastly, the on-board camera mic (again, the best unidirectional mic you can afford). The camera mic is LEAST desirable in that it picks up ALL of the field sound, not just the person interviewed. I prefer hard-wired lavs, for they are the most consistent source of sound recording.

TIME: Try to make sure you have *enough time* to do a proper interview in your preferred location. If you have 10 questions but only 10 minutes in your spot, you're in deep trouble. You'll have to move to another location and explain *why* on screen. *Give yourself time.*

TIME OF DAY: Having enough time also means shooting at the *right time of day*. Beware of midday when it's hot and the sun is often most intense. If it's in bright sunlight, turn the person around so their face is shaded. If it's a big setup, use a framed silk. Or put everyone in even shade.

WEATHER: Weather conditions can wreak havoc too. My first shoot in India decades ago was in blistering 110 degree heat. So, most of my interviews were shot early in the morning or at dusk, when I had better light and the temperature was bearable. Some interviews were done inside with bounce and fill light. Know that cold can present problems too - for the equipment, crew and subjects.

PAUSES: If you are the off-camera interviewer (who will not be seen or heard) then make sure the subject being questioned understands they need to provide a short pause before and after their answers. These pauses provide editing space to cut right to their response without your question heard off-camera interfering.

MAKE THE PERSON COMFORTABLE: I've worked many times with people who have never been interviewed before. They are usually nervous or apprehensive. Talk with them, put them at ease, try to listen to their concerns. The more relaxed you are, the more they'll be too.

BEWARE THE LONG ANSWER: I've worked with many ministers, who can give a 3 minute answer to what should be a 30 second response. Long answers are hard to cut together, and if you allow people to ramble, you've lost control of your interview. So, I will preface the shoot by telling the subject that we're looking for brief answers: 30-60 seconds. I will also coach them that using my question to *start* their answer works well too, i.e., make complete statements whenever possible. And, finally, if they have a good answer that is a bit long - but still excellent in content - I will sometimes ask them to rephrase their answer, getting them to try again with a shorter length. That way I have choices between both the long and short responses.

NIGER, WEST AFRICA

A shoot in the sub-Saharan African nation of Niger proved to be one of the most interesting interview setups I've ever shot.

My good friend, Dr. Dan Lucero, was to be interviewed for what became an award-winning documentary project, *Niger: Under the Umbrella of Islam*. We were on-location in the capital city of Niamey. Sunrise in that part of Africa arrives around 6-6:30 a.m. each day. I met Dan at the banks of the river near our hotel, and we began shooting around 7 a.m., in golden time, the best light (besides sundown) of the day. Over Dan's shoulder were the wet sand bars of the Niger. It was early, quiet, with few distractions. And the weather at that time of the morning was still relatively cool.

Just as I was asking Dan his very first question, a local fisherman - right out of the pages of *National Geographic*, and who was in the camera frame over Dan's shoulder - moved closer to us to watch our interview. He was perhaps 100 yards (30 meters) away. I was worried that if the fisherman moved at any time during the setup with Dan, we'd have to reshoot. My concern was over issues of continuity later when we edited: Now you see the fisherman in the shot, now you don't.

Instead, the fisherman, sitting on his hollowed-out wooden boat, stayed glued to the exact same position for the next 30 minutes without moving. He was present and still during the entire interview, for he must have been curious as to what we were doing. He became a perfect "extra" for our shot. It was as if we'd called "Central Casting" asking for an African fisherman to be placed perfectly in frame that day.

•

INTERVIEW BASICS

When conducting interviews, I'm constantly thinking of ways to edit the content. Through instinct, editing experience and homework (knowing my topic), I can tell when a sound bite from a person will help my story, or not. Give me three to four really good, solid responses, then I will have elements to put the piece together - especially if I have supporting visuals.

Often I will tell a person: "Give me a good start and a good finish. I'll take care of the middle with the rest of your comments."

Then I give them a nice smile.

RELEASES: Although I prefer written releases (and so do the producers and lawyers), I have had good success with doing on-camera video releases BEFORE I start the actual Q&A period. I will ask the cameraman to roll record, then will speak loud enough to be heard off-camera what the time and date is of the interview. Next, I'll ask the subject for permission to conduct the interview, ask them to spell their name, tell what their title and job is...and away we go with the interview.

I have *never* had a person refuse to do an interview through a *verbal release*, whereas, whenever I hand them a *written* release to sign, they sometimes hesitate, wanting to read the release before signing. I also use a video release for groups, putting everyone in the shot, then asking them *en mass* for their permission. It has worked well repeatedly. And the beauty is, if the interview is used by other editors, the release remains on the submitted tape or memory card.

LAST QUESTION: One other tactic I repeatedly use comes near the end of the interview. I will ask the subject, **"is there anything we've missed? Anything you'd like to share that we haven't covered?"** Out of the blue, people will express something that was on their hearts or minds that we hadn't covered.

Nine times out of ten, it's usable or valuable.

B-ROLL: Time and again, I am constantly thinking of the *visuals* to match the interview, i.e., supporting footage that will enhance the story. That's part of *Show & Tell* to me. **The interview TELLS me the story. The cutaway footage SHOWS me.**

The visuals (show) should outweigh the narration and interviews (tell). Film, television and video is a VISUAL medium. Words bring information, but **pictures have impact**, remembered long after the spoken word fades away or is forgotten.

INTERVIEW TIPS BY THE NUMBERS

1. Remember that just *one person* can often lead to other subjects who may shed light on your story too. Ask people who else they know or can suggest as interesting or authoritative on your topic or story.

2. Find a *good background.* As soon as you walk into a room or survey a site, look for the right, appropriate background or setting to shoot your interview. Standing or sitting someone in a location that enhances the story or topic brings great value to your production and its themes. A great setting helps tell your story too.

3. Allow *space* between the subject and the background, at least three to six feet. No one likes to see a professor interviewed with book cases crammed up behind their shoulders or an executive standing in front of a flat wall. Space allows the subject depth and definition, room for lighting and cuts down on unflattering shadows.

4. Place your subject away from *bright windows* behind them.

5. Using *natural or available light* from the side or behind the camera to light the interview is possible, but be careful of mixed light between outdoor and indoor.

6. Bring *blue gels* for daylight correction so that the color temperatures can be matched.

7. Place the camera at or just below the subject's *eye level.*

8. Grab focus on their *eyes.*

9. *Frame* the subject on either the right or left 1/2 or 1/3 side of the screen.

10. Unless they are doing an on-camera presentation with a defined purpose, have them look *off-camera* to the interviewer. The viewer then becomes a *participant* to the interview, as if they were sitting in with you listening and watching.

11. Place the interviewer *close* to the camera.

12. Think of the background as *supporting cast* never meant to upstage the subject, but complimenting their words and story.

13. Indoors, the subject should be lit *brighter* than the background.

14. Clip the lapel microphone (lavaliere) on the *side* of the subject *closest to the direction the person will be speaking.*

15. *Hide* dangling cords or cables with gaffer tape.

16. If using a shotgun mic, make sure it is *not visible* in the frame.

17. Consider using a *c-stand* with an arm and knuckle to place the interview microphone in a solid, placed position. Remember to put a sandbag on the legs of the stand for support and balance.

•

INTERVIEW TACTICS FROM PROS

"From a very young age my parents taught me the most important lesson of my whole life; they taught me how to listen. They taught me how to listen to everybody before I made up my own mind. When you listen, you learn. You absorb like a sponge and your life becomes so much better than when you are just trying to be listened to all the time."

- *Steven Spielberg, film director*

"Think conversationally. You are the representative for the people who can't be there in the room with you. What would they want to know just meeting the person you are interviewing? And if you can take a conversational tone, you will relax the person you are interviewing and get a better interview."

- *Martha Cotton, Plymouth Rock Studios*

"When directing real people in interview situations, try to direct them with replacement actions, instead of 'don't do this' direction. For example, an executive might have their hands in their pocket. If you say 'don't put your hands in your pocket', they will focus on that instead of the message - so their delivery will not be as good, and they'll be uncomfortable with their hands. Instead say, 'We've got the camera framed at your waistline, so please keep your hands above your belt, so we can see your gestures.' This gives them something positive to do that reinforces the message they are focused on."

- Don Hancock, Performance Communications

"Unless on-camera talent can talk directly to the camera, interviews should be looking slightly off-camera (I find it's more authentic to be listening in on someone telling another person their story).

"Use b-roll (cutaway footage) to bring out the story. Talking heads are boring and your audience will get lulled to sleep. Let visuals heighten the tone of the interview.

"Think about editing as you interview. It's easier to get a concise sound bite than to 'frankenstein' (cutting various bites of sound together) a long rambling statement."

- Steve Taylor, Digital Spatula

"Always end your interviews with the following two things:

"1. ASK: Is there anything I have not asked you that you want to share with me?

"2. RECORD: 60 Seconds of Audio of just the silence of the environment you're in....'Room Tone' to use in editing the interview."

-Aron Ranen, filmmaker-instructor

"Take special care in getting quality interviews. Good audio, close enough framing, limited visual distractions - a professionally done interview marks the difference between amateurs and pros in news production. If you can, place the subject against a story-related background. Then use only the sound bites you need. Interviews should not only move the story forward with more information, they should especially capture the emotions of the people involved.

"Comments should be short and concise. This will help you better remember the facts and emotion of the event, and might even be useful for a news report. Be sure to write down the people's names with correct spelling and titles, which will be important if any is used on the news. Keep the person within four feet of the camera. If in manual focus, zoom in and focus, then zoom out before recording.

Try to reduce background sounds as much as possible, and remember to have the light source behind the camera."

- Stan Jeter, CBN News

"Have anyone who appears on camera sign a release - ideally you would get them to sign it BEFORE rolling cameras on an interview, especially if you're worried the interview might not go well."

- Don Swaynos, editor-filmmaker

CHAPTER 3 REVIEW: INTERVIEWING

1. The best questions often come from the previous answer.
2. If you are only thinking of your next question, then you are failing as a filmmaker, interviewer and communicator.
3. People will tell you most anything if you listen closely.
4. Use Tell, Describe, Explain, Talk...and, perhaps, "someone told me..."
5. Do you want this FAST or GOOD?
6. Always leave a room as good - or better - than you found it.
7. One of the pitfalls of most any interview - including the sit-down - include *distractions*.
8. To cover a group interview really requires, at the minimum, two cameras.
9. Having as much control over the physical room is crucial to the interview's success, whether in front of or behind the camera.
10. Last question: "is there anything we've missed? Anything you'd like to share that we haven't covered?"
11. The interview *tells* me the story. Cutaway footage *shows* me.
12. Did you bring the *Spinelli Lens*?

CHAPTER 4: COMMUNICATION

Lost in Translation

•

"A relationship, I think, is a lot like a shark, you know? It constantly has to be moving forward, or it dies. And I think what we got on our hands is a dead shark."

- *Woody Allen, actor-director*

(Annie Hall, 1977)

Working on a shoot, show, segment, or media project is a lot about relationships. You're thrown in together for a common cause - to create a film, television, documentary or video piece (hopefully) of quality.

If you don't communicate, you've got a dead shark on your hands.

The whole process really is about teamwork and open lines of information. While there are plenty of one man (or woman) bands in film and television, communication still must be made with key contacts, other crew members and supporting players. No matter your talents, the diverse abilities to write, produce, direct, shoot, edit, act, narrate, run sound, fetch coffee, hold a boom mic, load tape, drive the van, make labels plus distribute and exhibit are more than most any single person usually can, and will, accomplish on any given project.

That means you're going to be working with other people 90% of the time. Hopefully, they possess creative, technical, organizational and dramatic abilities to enhance the project.

To be certain, **production is a collaboration**. From soup to nuts, it's a collective band of people working together to realize an artistic, technical or creative goal. The purpose is to produce a show, segment, dvd, webisode, documentary or commercial with the best of coordination, production, effort and actions possible.

Sometimes that work is for a network, agency, client or a company. Clients and bosses have great expectations, goals and requirements, because they are the ones funding the project or providing the vision for the content and delivery. In the end, it's often their message, product or brand being interpreted through media. So, they will have professional demands, and rightly so.

Because production is a collaboration, the creative process requires clear communication. This involves making sure everyone is on the exact same page and in agreement, with proper adjustments made along the way. There will be many times when few are on that same proverbial page, which is why producers get fired, directors are replaced, a cinematographer walks off a set or an actor sulks in their trailer.

These are called *creative differences*. And such tête-à-tête conflicts are legendary in the film and television industry. They may happen to you, too.

But this chapter really is not about creative differences. It's about communication: Making sure everyone involved is rowing the boat at the same time, on the correct stroke and heading in the right direction.

Communicating is about timely decisions, solid plans, achievable goals, genuine intentions and straightforward actions being properly articulated before, during and after a shoot or project.

Clear communication should be the mandate from first idea to final delivery. Far too often miscommunication is the curse for scores of media projects. And, unfortunately, failure is inevitable when people are slow to call, e-mail or speak up during the project process.

Other than money and ego, nothing can scuttle a shoot better than a lack of clear, straightforward communication. In my filmmaking experience, lack of communication has consistently been the proverbial thorn that has caused the most pain - big projects and small shoots, freelancer or staff.

Tackle the communication problem well - consistent, regular and upfront on the stream of information and responsibilities - and your next shoot will flow much more smoothly and successfully.

•

MALAWI, EAST AFRICA

Years ago, in Africa, I saw a very accomplished English film writer-director, Bart Gavigan, provide an excellent example of just what good, proper communication among a director and his crew was truly all about.

Gavigan and I were shooting at the same faith-based event with a dynamic, inspirational German speaker, Reinhard Bonnke, in the southern Malawian town of Blantyre. Each night the African crowd would grow, until by the last day of the event, a Sunday, the crowd was easily more than 150,000 people gathered in a large, open field.

Our small TV crew was assigned to cover the speaking for a USA broadcast series. We accomplished the shoot with just two cameras due to budget factors and local conditions. Concurrently, Bart's European team, perhaps 6-7 crew members, were shooting a separate, but very challenging dvd project at the same event. Their project was designed to be equal parts teaching video and motivational media piece featuring Bonnke. Bart's group had brought their own digital gear, and, during the course of the week's schedule, were shooting a number of extra special feature segments off-stage and in-town.

The entire group - TV show, dvd project and event staff - were staying at the same hotel in central Blantyre. During the evening, as my colleagues Dario, Tom, Alan, Derek and I would eat dinner in the restaurant, Bart's crew would often be seated just a table or two away.

Each night, after finishing-up their meal, Bart would then spend about 15-20 minutes with his crew going over what that particular day had accomplished. The team would weigh-in about what had gone right, wrong or could be improved upon. No matter their role or position, every crew member had the freedom and permission to speak up. Sometimes the issues discussed would involve equipment or shooting style appropriate for the next day's shoot.

With an easy going manner, Bart would continue to ask questions, give feedback, make adjustments, then brief his group about who they'd be interviewing the next day and what footage they'd be capturing, plus well into the week. He'd go over schedules, when a small (or large) production or logistical detail might prove problematic or need clarifying.

As I carefully watched and listened each night, I eventually realized that Bart was expertly conducting what the media industry often calls a "post mortem", which is a meeting at the end of the day (or project) to discuss what worked, failed or could be better improved on.

Such a closed meeting is when all the players - great or small - are gathered together, providing a proper, open forum to be briefed, ask questions, listen and, sometimes, vent.

***Post mortems* should be a staple of life on any production - period.**

Why? Because these gatherings provide a vital, necessary opportunity for everyone - staff, crew, management, talent, creatives - to recognize, speak and weigh-in about the project process.

•

COMMUNICATE

The art and science of communication is so much easier in a digital age than when many of us started in the late 1970s. Just having a smart cell/mobile phone alone cuts down on confusion, allowing for constant updating and dialog.

In the "old days" there were basically three ways to keep in touch: in person, via mail or by phone - that was about it. We were overjoyed when the fax machine was invented, for just the immediate ability to transmit pages of a budget, agreement, script, memo or document across borders, and the world, cut down on prep, speeding the flow of information, negotiation and consensus.

Today's cutting edge computers, web, texting and cell phones have changed that dynamic immeasurably; now communication happens in seconds, not hours, days, weeks or months. Yet communication still remains a thorny problem on far too many productions. Why? Because people still fail to actually *talk to each other*, and that means everyone, from producer to PA.

But there are other missing communication issues beyond just mere logistics that are rarely addressed, and they can prove to be terribly lethal, too: **unexpressed expectations, role definitions and hidden goals**.

•

THE CONGO, CENTRAL AFRICA

Years back, I produced, directed and shot a very difficult video on-location in Central Africa. Featured was an ambitious building project that gathered 70+ volunteers from American churches, all of whom paid their own way to the Congolese capital city of Kinshasa. Over three strenuous weeks this large team built a church, a medical clinic and a elementary school on a vacant field.

These were hard-working, dedicated people pitching in to do something worthy and honorable for a good cause - providing spiritual, medical and educational assistance for people in need.

My assignment was to serve as the director-cameraman for the video project, and to document this large team's building work, block by cinder block. I shot lots of construction footage, conducted interviews, covered the project from foundation laying to raising the roofs. Then we flew the very long, tiring journey back to the USA, crammed into a packed Sabena jet.

The client who commissioned my professional services, and paid for my services, had indicated from the very start that his goal for the video was to enlist more volunteers. His vision was to raise-up scores of dedicated people (like the 70+ volunteers I had traveled with) to build more churches, schools and clinics across Africa and, also, to other developing nations as well.

His intentions expressed to me, I highlighted the values of volunteering in my shooting, scripting and editing of the final video. The narration featured how building for the less fortunate was a worthwhile cause, proved inspirational and often impacted both the volunteer and the recipient. Interviews shot in the field (literally) described the joy and motivation of getting dirty and helping.

When I was nearly done with the video, I showed the client rough cuts, let him tweak the script a bit and make further suggestions. My gut feeling was that we were finishing strong, that this was going to be a very heartfelt, inspirational video.

The finished project was a solid ten to twelve minute piece produced for a reasonable price. Video delivered, I moved on to start work on other media projects believing I had accomplished the stated goals, and that the client would be pleased.

A few weeks later, just before duplication and distribution, I checked back to find out how a brief showing had gone. The client had played a show copy to a very important, influential church leader - and a good friend of his - for his feedback, reaction and advice. After the showing, that leader turned to my client and said, "nice video. But it's never going to raise any money."

My client was now very upset that his finished video - one that was clearly aimed at *volunteer recruitment* - was not going to be a big money maker too.

Why not? Because he *never* indicated in our conversations - at any point in the production process - that the additional goal of his video was *to raise money*. For the entire two months that we'd worked on the project - from core idea to travel to shooting to scripting to rough cut to final edit - the client had never once expressed his desire for the video to raise funds.

Frustrated, and a bit stunned, I gently told him so, mentioned my disappointment at the lack of communication, but it really didn't matter. Because he firmly believed that I should have - through osmosis or the psychic ability to read minds - discerned that his end goal was fundraising. When push finally came down to shove, the client was going to side with the church leader, who *was* correct in his assessment that the video was hitting a different target.

The video achieved little, went nowhere, a dismal failure. Good money spent editing in an impressive Hollywood edit suite had failed miserably to hit the true mark. My professional reputation took a hit, with some damage done - all because of a client's lack of communication.

As they say, **"success has many fathers. But failure is an orphan."**

•

WISHES & GOALS

Today, I am, of course, older and a bit wiser. Do you know how I would have approached that African church building video project now? Do you know what I ask present (and future) clients when I have a first exploratory meeting to lay the groundwork, to determine the stated nature of their project?

Now I ask the client:

- What do you want this project to accomplish?
- When the screen goes black, what should viewers think, feel or do?
- What action do you want them to take? Cry? Applaud? Be overwhelmed? Informed?
- Should they write, call, e-mail, volunteer, go to the web?
- Are they to write a check, give a gift, get on an airplane?

As the client answers those questions (or not) - because in the beginning things can be somewhat fuzzy - we make sure to WRITE DOWN THEIR GOALS.

From time to time, as the project process evolves or changes, we will return to those goals and expressed wishes. Later, near the end of the project when things might get tense and complicated, with everyone just wanting to get the piece finished, those written objectives from the beginning will become vitally important.

The goal is to keep checking back, just to make sure everyone is still on the same page.

Communication cuts down on surprises, minimizes frustration and clears confusion or misunderstanding. In fact, good communication often sees surprises before they will appear.

•

PREP MEETING

Throughout the 80s and 90s I traveled the world frequently, often gone three months a year flying 100k miles annually. Over the course of the *Unreached People* documentary series I booked four cameramen across four years - Steve, Randy, Jimmy and Sergio.

Before hiring each of these cameramen for a series of extremely long trips and productions, I would meet with them, have lunch and talk about what they should expect on journeys to Europe, Asia, Latin America or Africa.

I was prepping them for the assignment. This exploratory lunch was part of a good communication process: face-to-face over an hour or two I could explain the purposes of the upcoming shoots, about the clients, possible interviews, weather and shooting conditions, logistics, itineraries, equipment, hotels, meals, per diem, transport...a myriad of little but important things. Over those four years, we encountered few, if any, problems that occurred on our shoots, because most of the issues that cropped up had already been explored at that first lunch. Crew and director were usually on the same page, which is vitally important (especially when traveling).

What I also learned from those first crew meetings was that a phone call can only do so much. Today, sending an e-mail may be a great first start, but nothing replaces a face-to-face meeting over a cup of coffee or a plate of food. If that's not possible due to conflicting schedules or logistics, then some type of conference - even on speaker phone with all the proper players connected - brings everyone together to hash-out possible scenarios and issues early on.

Talk to each other before the shoot or heading to the airport.

State the goals, expectations and any sundry list of logistical objectives before your production starts. Communicate role definitions, shooting style, interviews, b-roll, who does what. Far too often plane tickets are purchased, people pack their bags, grab gear and then head to the shoot. That's when, too often, the real communication begins, usually at the physical production or airline gate. Unless a team has worked together seamlessly for many years, lack of upfront communication can turn into a recipe for disaster.

In my experience, ***early*** **communication beats** ***late*** **communication nine times out of ten.**

•

COMMUNICATION TIPS BY THE NUMBERS

1. **Whenever possible, deliver bad news personally - either by phone or face-to-face.** How you say NO speaks volumes about your integrity and character. *Yes* is easy. *No* is difficult, and is often avoided due to fear, apprehension and negative expectations. Unless the person is on assignment in Tajikistan and cannot be reached, try to call or meet people to deliver bad news. That way the other person can hear your voice, better understand your meaning and ask follow-up questions that bring clarity and closure to the situation. Be a professional...and genuinely kind. Resorting to an e-mail, voice mail or texting has become the easy, casual, insincere way out - not the correct way.

2. **Deal memos** - usually one page long - are perfect for engaging people's services for a shoot or project. Spelling out a crew member's role, pay rate, how other ancillary expenses will be covered and specific days of working cuts down on confusion and misunderstanding.

3. **If it's a simple shoot, even if booked by phone, still confirm with an e-mail (or if necessary, a text).**

4. **Be clear to staff, crew and talent about how long a shoot is expected to go.** Trying to cram a two day shoot into a one day setup is poor planning and producing. If you expect a very long production day, tell everyone involved upfront so they can plan. It's called courtesy.

5. **Never write something in an e-mail that you wouldn't be willing to say publicly.** Leave all negative words or opinions for actual conversations. Once you hit *send*, your e-mail is beyond your control forever and jetting it's way into cyber space. You have no idea beyond your original recipient(s) who will receive your e-mail, or how others will perceive or use it. **Your written words live for an eternity, and might come back to haunt you (and your career).**

6. **Be very careful what you post on any social networking site.** If you expect to be considered a professional, then racy, inappropriate pictures on your *My Space* page or odd comments on your *Facebook* wall could easily undermine your career. *Twittering* negative, caustic updates about the crazy shoot you're on in real time can come back to bite you too. Be careful what you write, post or comment on any public domain site.

7. **Answer you messages and e-mail in a timely manner.** Within 24 hours for business e-mails and phone messages, same day if possible. 48 hours for personal e-mails.

8. **If you've promised someone an answer by a specific time or day - and the deadline will be missed - contact the person.** Tell them what you know, and when you expect to have an answer. Usually, they will appreciate that you took the time to update them.

•

COMMUNICATION TACTICS FROM PROS

"Always ask yourself - what do I know and who needs to know it? Nothing can ruin a shoot faster than a bottleneck in the information flow."

- Lisa Swain, film professor, Biola University

"With your crew...talk about your philosophy and strategy before going out. Get on the same page."

- Steve Taylor, Digital Spatula

"If you fluff a take, let everyone know - it's harder to fix when everyone has left."

- Derek Murray, Cfan

CHAPTER 4 REVIEW: COMMUNICATION

1. If you don't communicate, you've got a dead shark on your hands.
2. Production is a collaboration.
3. Clear communication should be the mandate from first idea to final delivery.
4. *Post mortems* should be a staple of life on any production - period.
5. Beware of unexpressed expectations, role definitions and hidden goals.
6. "Success has many fathers. But failure is an orphan."
7. Communicating cuts down on surprises, minimizes frustration and clears confusion or misunderstanding.
8. Talk to each other *before* the shoot or heading to the airport.
9. *Early* communication beats *late* communication nine times out of ten.

CHAPTER 5: DIRECTING

Directing Traffic

•

"Anybody can direct a picture once they know the fundamentals. Directing is not a mystery, it's not an art. The main thing about directing is: photograph the people's eyes."

- John Ford, legendary director

(Stagecoach, The Quiet Man, The Grapes of Wrath)

In many respects, what John Ford is saying is that directing is not really a difficult role to fill or a tough task to perform. Naturally, it requires intelligence, creativity and knowledge. One must possess the talents to lead a team and express one's vision, for each are essential elements to shooting, guiding and finishing your project.

Plus, never underestimate the basic abilities to work with people, including those being interviewed or who are presenting. That's extremely important, because few directors (or anyone for that matter) in this day and age can afford to throw temper tantrums, be disagreeable or prove difficult to work with.

Directors are required to communicate with lots of people, from the lowest grip to the highest paid actor. And they must have a sense of the entire story, from start to finish, fade up to fade down. Ultimately, it's their mandate and responsibility to fill that screen with sights and sounds that engage, inspire, entertain, inform or provoke. But, in the end, it's the practical realities of production that are constantly being weighed against artistic sensibilities too.

It must be noted that the role of a director can be distinctly different based on the narrative form being shot, divided between *fiction* or *non-fiction*. (Sometimes there is a blend of both forms.)

For example, a cinema director working within the realm of fiction works from the blueprint that is a *screenplay*. Such a creative document guides the shooting process, but it is also the director's artistic vision (staging, shot selection, camera placement, casting, design) and interpretation of that script (along with dramatic performances), ultimately, that shapes the movie. The cinematic form really doesn't matter, whether Independent, Hollywood, Art House, Bollywood or Third cinema (liberation).

Unless the form is experimental - where improvisation and long, unedited takes are the essential ingredients - fiction films primarily rely on screenplays and scripts.

By contrast, in non-fiction storytelling, the task of the director requires certain artistic, exploratory skills that are unique - in some ways - from his/her counterpart in fiction. The director in documentary or non-fiction often works with amateurs - though not always - in front of the camera. Throughout the production process, the director's tasks include asking questions, conducting interviews and selecting cutaway (b-roll) footage to illustrate the spoken word and to enhance the story.

Sometimes the director is also the cinematographer too, which is usually rare in fiction (except for low budget Independent Film). There might be re-enactments involved, graphics, photos, bought or donated footage and efx - both visual and sonic. To my mind, non-fiction has a far greater range of styles and possibilities than narrative fiction, because the array of genres (sports, biography, news, science, music, politics, nature, etc.) are almost unlimited.

The process of production is a continuing evolution that takes various twists and turns based on what the contributors along the way may suggest, state or provide. Perhaps there are more interviews to shoot, additional story elements to consider, with details and information that arrive later in the production timeline.

In so many ways, **non-fiction adds layers to a story because the form is a journey to be taken unto itself, a work in progress.** Documentaries, as we've discussed, are often *organic* in that they grow in the hot house that is preparation and production, forming and developing over time.

There are exceptions to this organic rule. For example, *corporate video* may require a solid script, for the business or organization has certain goals to achieve. *Commercials* and *promotional* pieces require tight scripting too, for there are time factors (30 seconds/60 seconds) and response formulas that come strongly into play. Screen time proves to be precious.

However, directors in non-fiction still work, essentially, with people, both in front of and behind the camera. But those in front are rarely there to perform, per se, but to tell a part of the overall story. It's the subject's role to express their opinions on a topic or to provide eyewitness accounts of a person, time, event or place. They may be interviewed to share their specific story or background in ways that help define the narrative more clearly.

What part of that story to be presented in the final program is up to the creativity, vision, judgement and sensibilities of the director - and the strengths or weaknesses of the subjects interviewed.

Yes, there is a script involved, along with research (very important). And that script changes as fresh interviews are recorded, essential elements are investigated and diverse topic paths are explored. But when a full script is not possible, as we've explored, a *shot list* is a good place to start too. Such a list is often more than enough to create individual themes and story sequences that will all be tied together at the end (hopefully).

Of all the creative, managerial and technical roles I have performed in film, television and media production (producer, writer, camera, sound, production mgr), it is *directing* that gives me the greatest joy and satisfaction. Especially when working with people I respect and admire on a show, story or location that truly interests me - and perhaps an audience too.

The director's job taps my creativity and artistry, challenges my flexibility and adaptability, requires me to make key decisions and judgements involving time, budget, lighting, sound, location and shot selection. And I get to work face-to-face with wonderful, intelligent, interesting people on-camera, often coaxing unique performances or comments from them. That is fulfilling and constantly rewarding - whether on the back side of the world...or across town.

Directing is hard work, but fun and creatively fulfilling.

•

HAITI

To this day, the most difficult shoot I've ever directed in my career occurred in Haiti. I was hired at the last minute by a reputable production group in Hollywood to replace another field director for a investigative project on voodoo practices. The segment was part of a larger two hour Emmy-nominated TV special that aired on *A&E Network*.

Grabbing my bag, reading my notes and the voodoo books handed to me, I headed to Miami just three days after getting a phone call from the executive producer. A day later, I found myself landing in fiercely hot Port-au-Prince, which is like stepping into the "Africa of the Caribbean" due to the small island nation's immense poverty and dirty conditions.

Haiti, however, has a raw beauty about it in the rural locations, but truth be told, the country has been given over to the devil - literally. The saying in Haiti is that the country is 90% Catholic, but 100% voodoo. Believe them, for they are entirely correct.

My assignment was to accompany a small group of African-American voodoo believers who had journeyed from the East Coast of America to Haiti. Their mission was to gather sacred herbs, visit at the local peristyles (worship houses) and to travel up-country to a mystical waterfall for fertility rituals. To cover all of these events, the production company back in Los Angeles had already hired the local Haitian CNN news crew, a freelance cameraman and sound man. They were my team (and a good one) for about a week of shooting.

The greatest challenge as the field director - and this is where the difficulty of non-fiction directing comes into play - was that I was not known by the voodoo practitioners before the shoot nor was I trusted when I arrived. I was replacing someone else at the last minute, another field producer, who they already knew, liked and accepted completely. She had befriended them while shooting and producing an earlier USA segment at their home sanctuary. At the last minute, she had an unexpected emergency come up, so I was called, briefed and hit the airport.

Because I was new and unknown to everyone, distrust of me infused the group, which was terribly secretive and paranoid from the start. Dressed all in white, the small group of about ten bought their herbs at the local market in the capital city, and then, while chanting and singing, pounded them into potions near the hotel garden each morning, a chore they were required to perform as part of their sacred duties.

Directing this voodoo band was the "mambo", their spiritual leader and high priestess, who was a large African-American woman dressed in white too. Her name was Angélá, and she exerted full spiritual control over her devotees. Angélá would not rise before about 10 a.m. each morning, and would not appear until after she was makeup ready for the interviews and production shots. Her tardiness, which was not to be trespassed, was a wrench thrown into the grinding machinery of our tight production schedule.

What the mambo spoke was the authoritative word. Her commands were carried out faithfully by her minions. And as field director I was engaged in a constant tug-of-war with her over the direction of the shoot and the ambitious schedule involved.

For example, she found out later our camera team had videotaped the herbal potion preparation, this done while she had been sleeping in one morning. I was asked straightaway to surrender the recorded tape. She had not been informed of this segment, she said, and her reason for requesting the footage was that the herbs we photographed were both sacred and secret, and not to be divulged on television. Hand-over the tape - or the shoot would be canceled. (Even though we had received permission beforehand - we thought - to shoot the herb process.) With little choice, I gave her the tape, which only had the potion ceremony recorded, thank goodness.

Money was a constant issue, as a production fee was to be paid to her group. I had brought them a company check for an amount agreed upon with the production company (before I had become involved). But beyond this initial payment, virtually every day a new money pitch was made by the mambo or another leader for some new voodoo ceremony or ritual their group could perform for another large fee. One colorful proposal was an offer to sacrifice a live bull on-camera, the ritual "only" costing $5000. But the local priest, naturally, needed a couple days notice to procure and prepare the large animal. I politely declined, as I knew the production company was on a limited budget already, and I didn't have $5000 in my pocket at the moment.

At different times each day, the schedule would be delayed or changed due to the whims and desires of the mambo. I would make our suggestions to help along the process of schedule and time constraints, but we marched to whatever beat I could negotiate with Angélá. All in all - other than the agreed segments to be recorded - we kept to our separate ways, while staying at the same hotel (the Montana) overlooking the city.

Every detail was difficult. Each setup and shoot required superb people and negotiating skills, plus ample loads of patience and kindness. I have never had to work so hard to get subjects to sit for interviews, to wait without frustration until they were ready, to understand and anticipate what might be coming next. My professional assignment had very little to do with film aesthetics, montage theory and the artistic exploration of where to place a camera.

It had come down to muddling through a very difficult shoot in a hot, faraway island nation with very strange people.

In the end, two big, important segments were recorded successfully, and both sequences turned out to be impressive.

First, we shot late one night at a raucous ceremony attended by the group, a full blown voodoo party in a peristyle on the outskirts of Port-au-Prince. Right out of *National Geographic*, it was a colorful swirl of pounding drums, gin drinking, energetic dancing, soulful chanting, demon worship and spiritual possession. As part of their animistic beliefs, voodoo practitioners invite the spirits (loas) to inhabit their bodies, taking control. When this happens - and believe me, this was no show - eyes roll back, bodies gyrate and physical shaking ensues. The process can go for minutes, or hours, until, at some point, the spirits leave and the believer re-enters the world around them. Our crew and I captured it all, most everything that moved, even though it was done very "seat of the pants." There was no grand plan as to who would do what, when, where or even how. Welcome to making-it-up as you go.

Our team finished up our part of the shoot around midnight for scheduling reasons, as we'd be into serious crew overtime if we'd stayed later. Word got back to us the next day that the rest of the voodoo group continued through most of the night, ending around 4 a.m. This was powerful visual and sonic material on tape, and exactly what the production company had sent me to go get. These ritualistic, African-themed music, dancing and spiritual sequences worked extremely well in the final *A&E* TV special.

The second major segment was much more problematic logistically, for it involved a difficult trip to a famous waterfall called "Saut d'Eau" in the green mountains just outside of Port-au-Prince. The arduous journey by 4 wheel drive was partly to worship at the falls but also designed so that a wife of a believer could bath in the waters, a practice dedicated to restoring her fertility. The woman had been unable to conceive children, and the trip to the waters was meant to heal her.

Driving perhaps 15 miles up the very windy hills took somewhere close to three hours due to the rough conditions and terrain. After we arrived in the small town nearby, the worshippers lit candles at the local Catholic church, then headed to the waterfall. For the next couple hours we captured cover footage as the group bathed in the waters, and, finally, the woman immersed herself in the pools overflowing from the waterfall's cascade.

At that point, things got extremely trippy. Through chanting and worship, she invoked the water loas and began slithering through the pools like a snake, her eyes rolling back into her head. Other believers came to rescue her, as she was close to drowning, mouth open, writhing in the water. Our cameraman captured it all, with me barefoot next to him assisting. Both of us rolled up our pants legs, getting into the water to shoot close-ups and various handheld shots. The entire sequence made the final edit, and was eerie, spiritual footage.

In the end, we as a crew - and I as director - were exhausted. The physical, logistical and spiritual tasks involved were tremendous and taxing. And the emotional challenges of negotiating most every little detail from start to finish with the mambo, Angélá, drained me emotionally as well.

Production finished, I left for the airport and the flight back to Miami, then L.A., as drained professionally and personally as I could possibly be. Field directing the voodoo shoot took about every ounce I had of patience, tenacity and perseverance. In the end, the shots were easy, for I had a great, experienced crew. It was the people and process that truly challenged me.

Welcome to directing.

•

ROLE OF DIRECTOR

Does the role of director involve time in the editing suite or reworking the script or fleshing out the shot list? Yes. Is the look and lighting critical? Of course. Everything a director does - negotiating, creativity, decision-making, camera placement, casting, story development, technical aspects, communicating, collaborating with crew, producers and talent - comes into play.

But a tremendous percentage of working as a director also comes down to the expert abilities one must possess in working with numerous people effectively from all walks of life, from top to bottom (just like I had to do in Haiti).

Master your people skills and decision-making, and you will be on the right track to success in your film, television, video and media projects.

•

HOLLYWOOD, CA

Years back, I was hired by my producing friend and colleague in New York, Brad Fuss, to shoot a behind-the-scenes segment in-studio with David Bowie for *ABC's In Concert*. The legendary rock singer was filming a music video for one of his upcoming albums. Our small television crew arrived one morning at *Hollywood Center Studios* near Santa Monica Blvd. Bowie's set was already beautifully lit, with the crew and cameras in place, every "extra" costumed and ready. As we arrived, the entire production was just beginning to start filming for that day.

While we shot our backstage part of the coverage, I was amazed at just how well every little detail for the music video was planned, scheduled and executed on Bowie's large set. Here it was 9 a.m., and they were already into physical production, an early call time unheard of at that hour for most music videos. The film crew was shooting with five Arriflex 35mm cameras, including one on a Chapman crane, two cameras on dolly tracks (pulled by camera assistants) and two handheld Steadicams on the sides. Elsewhere in the vast studio, technicians, set designers and painters were putting the finishing touches on other scenes for shooting later that day.

The atmosphere on Bowie's set was easy-going, everything right as rain. There was not an ounce of tension, trouble, frustration or conflict. It just flowed so seamlessly. The sense was that every crew member was going about their specific duties and responsibilities calmly and efficiently.

To this day, it was the most relaxed big production shoot I've ever worked on.

What I also remember most was the easy demeanor of the talented music video director, who was from England. He was, without a doubt, the calmest person in the entire room. The director exuded a quiet confidence that he knew exactly what he wanted, and had communicated his creative plans at every level of the production. That artistic vision was now being fully realized by way of a perfectly lit set that was covered extensively by multiple cameras run by professionals. Virtually every shooting angle was capturing the performances - the star, the band and the back up singers. Now and then the director would whisper a suggestion into the ear of a camera operator, or go over and talk with Bowie. But the whole shooting process all seemed so absolutely effortless...and very professional.

A confident, relaxed director - who knows exactly what he/she wants and has communicated their vision properly - should be the calmest person on almost any set.

That calmness creates a positive, productive atmosphere that spreads itself around to everyone involved, from the most important executive producer to the hardest working production assistant.

•

DIRECTING TACTICS FROM PROS

“Pickup a camera. Shoot something. No matter how small, no matter how cheesy, no matter whether your friends and your sister star in it. Put your name on it as director. Now you're a director. Everything after that you're just negotiating your budget and your fee.”

- James Cameron, director

“A subtle word may quiet a noisy director, but don't bank on it.”

- Derek Murray, Cfan

“I always like to think of the audience when I am directing. Because I am the audience.”

- Steve Spielberg, director

“In feature films, the director is God. In documentary films, God is the director.

“If it's a good movie, the sound could go off and the audience would still have a perfectly clear idea of what was going on.

"A good film is when the price of the dinner, the theatre admission and the baby-sitter were worth it.

"I don't understand why we have to experiment with film. I think everything should be done on paper. A musician has to do it, a composer. He puts a lot of dots down and beautiful music comes out. And I think that students should be taught to visualize. That's the one thing missing in all this. The one thing that the student has got to do is to learn that there is a rectangle up there - a white rectangle in a theater - and it has to be filled.

- Alfred Hitchcock, director

"I'm a storyteller - that's the chief function of a director. And they're moving pictures, let's make 'em move!"

- Howard Hawks, director

"One of the great things about being a director as a life choice is that it can never be mastered. Every story is its own kind of expedition, with its own set of challenges."

- Ron Howard, director

"A hunch is creativity trying to tell you something."

- Frank Capra, director

"A good director's not sure when he gets on the set what he's going to do."

- Elia Kazan, director

"A director is a lot like a general at war: Everything needs to keep moving forward."

- Chris Wilson, writer (Animal House)

"Directing is tone, and tone is the hardest thing to explain to someone. It's like how you know you're in love with somebody."

- Jason Reitman, director

"Directing is the ultimate 'all of the above'. You're the head coach, and like a head coach, your job is to create an atmosphere where all your collaborators, every department head, every worker, every actor, the writers if you're working with them, can do their best work around the common goal, which is the best movie possible from this material."

- Richard Linklater, director

"Part of the job of directing is being able to think fast on your feet, improvise and come up with some other idea that does what you wanted to do in the first place."

- Phil Alden Robinson, director

"For a director there are commercial rules that are necessary to obey. In our profession, an artistic failure is nothing; a commercial failure is a sentence. The secret is to make films that please the public and also allow the director to reveal his personality."

- John Ford, director

"Spielberg gave me just two tips about directing: First, change your shoes at lunch. Second, you'll figure it out."

- Tom Hanks, actor-director

"If you're a creative person, then creating is what you do, all the time, in every moment of your life. That desire is always there, to make something, paint something, take a photograph, act a scene, it's just a part of who you are."

- Dennis Hopper, actor-director

"You make a film to distract people, to interest them, perhaps to make them think, perhaps to help them be a little less naive, a little better than they were."

- Claude Chabrol, director

"It is only when I am doing my work that I feel truly alive."

- Federico Fellini, director

CHAPTER 5 REVIEW: DIRECTING

1. "The main thing about directing is: photograph the people's eyes. "- *John Ford*
2. Directors are required to communicate with lots of people, from the lowest grip to the highest paid actor. And they must have a sense of the entire story, from start to finish, fade up to fade down.
3. What part of that story to be presented in the final program is up to the creativity, vision, judgement and sensibilities of the director - and the strengths or weaknesses of the subjects interviewed.
4. Non-fiction adds layers to a story because the form is a journey to be taken unto itself, a work in progress.
5. Directing is hard work, but fun and creatively fulfilling.
6. A confident, relaxed director - who knows exactly what he/she wants and has communicated their vision properly - should be the calmest person on almost any set.

CHAPTER 6: DECISION-MAKING

Decisions, Decisions

•

"You're Marines now.

You adapt. You overcome. You improvise."

- Sgt. Thomas "Gunny" Highway (Clint Eastwood)

Heartbreak Ridge (1986)

The decisions you make in the field, on-set or in the studio are *critical* to the success of your story, segment, show, shoot or project. No matter the depth and greatness of your preparation, research and planning, as a filmmaker you will be challenged throughout your shooting day with split second decisions. Make the right ones - repeatedly and consistently - and you'll succeed.

Choose poorly, and you'll be constantly reshooting, gathering the wrong cutaway footage or heading-off to record more interviews because you just don't have enough material.

Please know, and realize, that every filmmaker from 1896 till today has made mistakes. We are all human, and the production process is demanding and difficult, filled with potholes and wrong turns. (But, on the positive side, there are plenty of successes too.)

In the end, we all make the best decisions we can based on the criteria we're presented with at a specific moment. It all comes down to time, budget, personnel, sunlight, script, performance, tension, shooting requirements, production constraints and a million other little - but crucial - details.

•

GUILIN, CHINA

I still remember a small, but critical decision I had to make in Guilin years ago. The crowded city is famous for its unique jagged peaks. Pick most any good guidebook of China, look up Guilin, and the region's peaks will be featured. They are majestic, beautiful and eerily unusual. They'd be perfect for a *Star Wars* movie.

On an overcast March morning our team was shooting there, we knew - I knew - we needed to be productive. We had just a single day to shoot, nothing more, before moving north to Beijing.

At breakfast in our hotel, my colleague, and Mandarin-speaking guide, Jon Davis, presented to our small documentary crew a basic plan for the day. The first possibility was to take a slow, winding boat tour down the Li River, whereby we could cover the Guilin peaks over the course of perhaps two to three hours. It was a picturesque, rambling, touristy ride straight out of *Travel Channel.*

The second option - Plan B - was to hire a local car to take us to a nearby village just out on the far outskirts of this large city. The goal would be to capture typical rural life in China, how most Chinese existed, in an area that resembled the countryside. An entire morning could be devoted for village production. The advantage of the village option, too, was that the driving distance was not too far, perhaps a twenty to thirty minute drive.

At that critical moment I weighed both options: Guilin peaks...or Chinese village life.

In my mind I considered how many Guilin peaks I'd possibly be using as director in a twenty minute documentary on Chinese culture and spiritual beliefs. I predicted, at most, one to two shots. The peaks were not truly essential to the story. Spending a whole morning on a boat ride might be fun and visual, but not productive or worthwhile to the storyline.

On the other hand, a full morning in a Chinese village had a great cultural upside: people living, working, farming and going about their daily lives seemed to present far more potential.

I chose the village.

Years later I still realize just how wise that little decision turned out to be.

Our three man crew drove to the edge of Guilin to a small village with perhaps a few hundred people. The famous peaks were still majestically perched out on the horizon, plus there were new crops in the field. A gushing stream ran through the little village, and as we arrived we found people hand washing their clothes in the cool water. Kids were playing outside the simple, battered homes. Women were busy doing household chores such as cooking, sweeping and tidying up. And, of course, the men were doing nothing - welcome to male behavior in the developing world .

After asking for permission to film, we spent the next few hours covering most everything that moved: kids, women, men, crops, peaks, washing, cooking, talking, game playing. We even found a children's graveyard further away, out in the fields, a sequence that proved illustrative in the overall research to show how the Chinese at that time were forced into having only one child, with boys desired most. This adherence and pressure - suspected issues of *infanticide* - had caused girl babies to be "done away" with quietly and privately. The gravestones were visual evidence of that horrific trend.

Choosing the village turned into two cassettes of good, valuable footage that was used repeatedly and successfully in the final program. I can still remember the specific shots and editing the rough cut prior to on-line mastering. The show had a bounty of excellent people shots, colorful village life and distinct footage of rural Chinese culture.

Looking back, the Guilin peaks would have accounted for, perhaps, 5-10 seconds of screen time, but hours of wasted time filming on a slow sailing river boat.

•

THE WILD GOOSE CHASE

Making tiny, critical decisions in a production will make or break you...and your project.

One of the large blocks of time in the non-fiction form is shooting interviews, which we explored in a previous chapter. The perfectly lit sit-down interview can easily take half a day. By the time you travel to the office, site or room, select the correct spot, setup lights, mic, shoot, tear down, then hustle to the next location on your shot list can take hours. And often - especially in news gathering - that interview only results in about 10-15 seconds on-screen - usually just enough time for a short sound bite for the story.

While important to most any project, interviews chew up time.

One of the dynamics you want to steer clear of is what I term "The Wild Goose Chase". This is usually a shoot that has been suggested by the client, a local representative or a sincere, but misguided producer who believes that certain footage, a subject or a shoot will turn into solid, worthwhile footage.

No matter one's experience, we've all ridden on *The Wild Goose Chase* at least one time or another.

•

PARIS, FRANCE

I can still remember shooting in Paris for the pilot episode of the PBS series *Traveling Lite*. The producer had setup a late night shoot at a chic dance club (*Les Bains Douches*) to show hip, club-going Paris. In theory, it was a great idea because it was certainly appropriate for a youth oriented travel show packed with advice on entertaining things to do and cool places to go.

Our crew arrived at the club well after dinner, perhaps 10 o'clock. The club had formerly been a bath house years before, that's where the term "Les Bains Douches" came from. At that hour of the evening - late for us, early for young Parisians - the club was virtually empty, so we were the only customers. After sitting for awhile and sipping on cold drinks, I asked the producer when the club was expected to start filling-up. Past 2 o'clock in the morning was his estimation. And the place would really start getting crowded about 3 a.m., he said. Not good.

Our already tired production crew would have to wait at least another three to four hours before shooting any "hip" footage in a packed dance club. To make matters worse, we were expected to be up at 7 a.m. the next morning for more filming. And it would take at least one hour later that night to drop everyone off at the two hotels we were staying in, which were in different *arrondissements* (districts) of Paris.

My quick decision was to save the crew (and evening) by shooting the host and hostess segments in a chic but empty side room of the club right away, even with no crowd yet. To make the shoot *feel* like a busy night club, I had crew members walk in front of the camera constantly, as if the hosts were speaking in a room packed with hundreds of energetic club-goers. The walk through shots gave energy to the scene.

Host segments shot, we then left for our hotels to get some much needed rest. On a separate night we shot at a second club (already packed around mid-evening). Then, in editing, we intercut dance floor footage from the second club with the original *Les Bains Douches* host setups. To my mind, dancing was dancing, especially when music was pulsating and strobe lights were blaring. I then added the sound efx of club and crowd noise.

The edited sequence looked, sounded and felt like it had all been shot on the very same evening in just one place.

It was a smart move. And no one knew the difference (except us) that the combined club footage was from two different locations and nights. Plus, we were in bed asleep by midnight that first evening.

•

These critical decisions point out the very practical thinking necessary for most any successful filmmaking: developing your keen abilities to roll with the punches as they arrive is essential. Adjusting and making timely choices - correct ones - are the tell tale signs of a confident filmmaker.

One of the keys is planning well, which allows you the wonderful freedom to be spontaneous.

Being well prepared cuts down on anxiety!

Decision-making is just as important as the sizzling script you've developed, the incredible shot depicting tension in your story between characters, a highly constructed chase sequence, or landing a big interview. Although, you could argue, each of these elements might be important in the scheme of story and production.

Correct decisions in the field will continually serve you...and your project.

Yes, making key decisions will mean mistakes. Know that you will make them. The best advice I can give? Learn from them. Try very hard not to repeat them. Use those mistakes to build experience and knowledge, honing your *instinct* for your craft.

Instinct will become that inner voice that guides you in the field, on the set and in the studio. That's when you know confidently what you want, what's right, what works and how these tiny elements (or large) will all fit together to create a successful sequence or segment. When you create, as a filmmaker, enough compelling sequences that can be stitched together seamlessly, you are well on the pathway to creating a solid story, segment or show.

Willingness to make mistakes is a sign of security. Every filmmaker has crashed and burned, so you are not alone. But you will never accomplish your mission by just sitting and doing nothing...or, truth be told, by always taking the safe, easy pathway. Wasting valuable time thinking through every single possibility to make every specific shot perfect rarely works. Unless you're the late, legendary director Stanley Kubrick, with all the time in the world as an auteur, what you shoot will never be completely perfect. But do try to make what you shoot as good as possible.

The ability to make quality, timely decisions as you go is paramount.

•

FILM SCHOOL

A few years ago I took a break at mid-career to return to college to pursue a Masters degree in Film Studies at Chapman University in

Orange, CA. This was becoming a hot film school acquiring a solid reputation, and is now considered *Top 10.*

I found myself surrounded by young, fledgling directors and cinematographers who were constantly working on student films and projects. Throughout the semester they'd be given assignments to shoot and tell a story in just 1 minute. Every shot was critical. Every frame of film precious. In fact, their film magazine (16mm) only held about three minutes of film. They were forced to make tight decisions or they would, literally, run out of film stock.

Because I was older (in my late 40s), I was recruited by a few student directors to be an amateur actor in their directing projects. It was a casting decision on their part - since there were few mature "actors" or subjects available to them - and I was a good guy willing to help.

Whenever I acted in student projects, I was amazed at the time it took these young directors to make decisions. The shot had to be perfect, the setup spot on, as the Brits would say. So much was given to the look of their film, that the acting and emotional parts were often neglected...including my part, but also others acting with me. The directors would stand there and think, ask questions, reframe, think again, then finally make a decision. Many times they were so into the shot *behind* the camera that they forgot about the performance *in front* of the camera.

This did not frustrate me at all, for the weight of the project and production was certainly not on my shoulders. I was there only to act, nothing more. So, I waited while cameras were placed, lights set and choices were kicked around between director and crew. Never did I try to direct, but instead stuck to my role, rarely if ever making a suggestion. After awhile, though, I learned to turn down these offers to act in the student projects because, invariably, I would be told the shoot would take only a few hours of my time.

But what should have taken a few hours took ages due to indecision, with shoots taking two to three times longer than anticipated.

•

INSTINCT

Once you develop an instinct for what you want - and how to achieve it - you will be freed mostly from indecision. Choices, good and bad, will hone that instinct. Stay true to your project vision, but sharpen your decision-making - doing so will help you achieve your goals.

Clint Eastwood, in my estimation, is a great example of a confident filmmaker who has some of the best directing skills going. True, he works in narrative fiction, armed with a script, great actors, crew, location and budget. But he knows, after decades, what it is that he wants and how to realize it up there on a big screen. It's been written that he often shoots a sequence in just one to two takes, maybe three. The director makes his set so comfortable that other actors knock out their lines while hardly noticing that the camera is rolling.

Eastwood knows his angles, setups and the process. When he has a good dramatic take in the film can that he likes, he might shoot a "safety" take, but usually moves on to the next setup in a workmanlike fashion. He "sees" his film in his mind and is able to translate his unique vision onto the screen, time and again. Winning multiple Academy awards and creating a prestigious body of film work are testaments to his abilities.

Confidence, including within the documentary or non-fiction realm, is a virtue. (Over confidence is not; it's called arrogance.) And that attribute will often rise to the surface from good, creative ideas - and solid decisions.

Indecision paralyzes a project. The sun is going down, there is only so much available light. The day is wasting. People are waiting. Costs are mounting. Time is precious.

Adapt, overcome, improvise.

•

DECISION-MAKING TACTICS FROM PROS

"There are no rules in filmmaking. Only sins! And the Cardinal sin is dullness."

- Frank Capra, director

"Endless takes because you don't know what you want frustrate talent and crew - while displaying your ineptness."

- Don Hancock, Performance Communications

"As a camera operator, when a director of photography or director changes their mind constantly and wants a different shot, just maintain a good attitude and make the change with no whining!! Maybe offer a suggestion or two (but not too much!!) on tweaking a shot to make it better."

- Michael J. Denton, network cameraman

"Pressure makes diamonds."

- Missouri Advertising Sign

"No excuses. No explanations."

- Julia Child, TV cooking host

"Great preparation allows you to be wonderfully spontaneous with less anxiety.

"Anxiety is the price you pay for an unprepared mind."

- Dr. Marty Cohen, Cohen-Brown Picture Company

CHAPTER 6 REVIEW: DECISION-MAKING

1. The decisions you make in the field, on-set or in the studio are *critical* to the success of your story, segment, show, shoot or project.
2. Being well prepared cuts down on anxiety!
3. Willingness to make mistakes is a sign of security.
4. The ability to make quality, timely decisions as you go is paramount.
5. Once you develop an instinct for what you want - and how to achieve it - you will be freed mostly from indecision. Choices, good and bad, will hone that instinct.
6. Confidence, including within the documentary or non-fiction realm, is a virtue.
7. Indecision paralyzes a project.
8. Adapt, overcome, improvise.

CHAPTER 7: BUDGETING

Money Sense

•

"This movie cost $31 million.

With that kind of money I could invade a country."

- Clint Eastwood, director-actor

By today's Hollywood standards, Eastwood's budget is actually rather frugal for a major motion picture. By the time a studio pays for film production (with producers, directors, stars, writers, crew, studio and locations), plus the enormous cost of marketing, prints and distribution, you're talking $100 million on average.

But Eastwood's right in that for $31 million you could send a small commando team to invade the tiny African nation of Equatorial Guinea, topple their dictatorship and install new democratic leaders. Don't believe it? Frederick Forsyth's great 1974 book on mercenaries for hire, entitled *The Dogs of War*, is just such a blueprint on the subject.

Filmmaking - whether film, television, digital or video - costs money.

Production guru, John Gaskin, who has worked on over forty movies, believes that money is the most important aspect of filmmaking. That the flow of financing trumps creative vision, high-priced talent, script and story arcs. The *Weekly Cost Report*, he contends, is more important than the dailies. When money dries up, so does the fuel for physical production and the various creative and technical services involved.

People, vendors, services and facilities have to be paid for.

Even on a much smaller scale, without project funds, how are you as a filmmaker or videographer going to achieve your goal of shooting and producing your story, documentary, video or film?

No matter the size of your project, create a budget.

To be clear, this chapter on budgeting is NOT about film financing, including where and how to secure independent funding for your next art nouveau short film or long form documentary.

What I can tell you is to **manage your production money wisely.**

No matter the source of your funding, create a realistic budget in advance. Itemize all of the line items where you expect to spend money. Break certain parts of the project timeline down to pre-production, production and post. Include mastering, duplication and delivery. Talent, crew, locations, travel, studio, vendors, gear, transport, out-of-pocket - get it all down and estimated. Plus, anticipate when funds will arrive, and in what amounts, i.e., *cash flow*. Then figure *who* and *what* needs to be paid *when*, in *what amounts*, and *how* (check, wire transfer, cash, credit card, direct deposit).

In my case 99% of the time, I have been fortunate to have a client, agency or sponsoring organization footing the production bill, whether for a single shoot in Newport Beach or two weeks to India and back. It has been my primary job as a producer, director or cameraman to estimate what the project would cost, create an itemized budget, get it negotiated and approved, create a basic deal memo or contract, then head off to do the actual shoot or project.

Usually, the greatest arguments have come down to money - the budget and costs - not the creative. (Though that can happen too, especially when there exist frayed lines of vision or communication.)

Putting Eastwood's $31 million movie aside, documentary, short film, television and video productions by their very nature are usually accomplished for a fraction of what a major film costs. Unless you are talking about a leading network TV show or recognizable cable special/series, the costs for single or two camera shoots are far less expensive based on smaller sized crews, reasonable gear, and fewer days in the field or studio. Another important factor is that, most often, the featured talent are subjects being interviewed on-camera who cost little or nothing for their opinions and reactions.

We're not talking Hollywood blockbusters, but small productions.

No matter the size, scope or cost of your project, budgeting still must be considered before starting most any production. That includes that one day shoot with a two man crew recording three cassettes along Bourbon Street in New Orleans during Mardi Gras.

In my case, I shoot overseas a lot - that's my specialty. My hard earned experience tells me that the very nature of foreign production consistently costs far more than domestic. Two or three times more. Major cities of the world can be very expensive. I remember having a lunch years ago in Tokyo that cost $50, for one person. Hotel rooms were $250 a night, a bargain at that time.

Ever paid for a hotel in Rio de Janeiro? Been hit up for overweight baggage in Hong Kong? Bought an airline ticket to Johannesburg? Flights, consecutive days in hotels, most every meal eaten out, crew rates and equipment fees, local transportation, travel time, insurance and bonding...it all multiplies and adds up, till it finally lands down there on the bottom line.

If your production includes shooting in separate locations across various countries, cities or provinces, then you need to anticipate your funding and estimate a budget. That even applies for basic shoots in the same town over a short period of time. Booking a good studio requires time, money and planning too. Sending your production team into the field or onto a set - near or far - without the proper financial support jeopardizes your crew, shoot, project and chances of success. It could all fall down like a house of cards.

How you estimate and track your budget is incredibly important to the very lifeline of prep and production. Budget also impacts post-production workflow, timelines and delivery.

•

WHERE TO START

Where to get started with an initial budget?

Research costs, even for in-town shoots, and expect them to be higher than what you had originally planned. Ask veteran line producers, production managers or crew coordinators who have experience in budgeting to help you formulate your budget right. That way you will create something based much closer to reality than wishful thinking.

If at all possible, try to add a *contingency fund* with an extra 10-15% cushion "just in case" - it will help. That way you're covered for an unexpected expense if and when it occurs.

Also, realize as you dive-in with costs, facts and figures that *no two film or video shoots are exactly alike.* There are few "apples versus oranges" comparisons. The two day shoot in Denver will be nothing like the four day shoot in New York, or a one week trip with a three person crew to Paris or Buenos Aires. Or the corporate shoot hiring a local crew in San Francisco. That's because documentary, video and film productions have so many variable factors that make each specific shoot and project uniquely different from another.

Here are some suggestions on creating a budget:

SOFTWARE: There are a number of excellent software programs available for scheduling and budget, including:

- *Movie Magic* (professional budgeting for film, television and media projects)
- *Show Starter* (entertainment projects)
- *AICP* (Association of Independent Commercial Producers)
- *Quicken/Quick Books* (basic accounting software you can use to categorize your budget, manage your cash flow, plus pay people, services and vendors in a timely manner)

At the very least, create a budget spreadsheet on *Excel* to guide your project. But the value of purchased software is that many programs include scheduling with the budgeting.

BUDGET LINE ITEMS: Break them down into categories based on the nature of your project. Most professionals start with pre-production, production and post:

- Treatment, Script or Screenplay
- Above-the-Line costs (producers, directors, actors, director of photography, narrator)
- Below-the-Line (camera crew, gaffers, grips, sound personnel, extra crew, makeup/hair. production managers & coordinators, production assistants, etc.)
- Travel, Lodging, Meals, Catering, Transport etc.
- Design, Sets, Scenery, Props
- Insurance, Bonding, Carnets
- Tape stock or Film stock (or both)
- Camera & Sound Equipment, Lighting, Generators, Gaffer Truck, Trailers
- Location Fees, Scouting, Permits
- Petty Cash, Out-of-pocket expenses, Advances
- Lab fees, Developing, Prints, Mastering
- Editors, Editing Software and Equipment, Efx, Sound mix, Music, Digital Intermediate
- Mastering, Duplication, Distribution

This is just a very basic list of possible categories to consider. Depending on the size and nature of your shoot, these specific line items can easily multiply into dozens more - or might be only four to five items at most.

To facilitate your budget, and depending on the formality of accounting systems, you may need to know about purchase orders, check requests, invoicing, wire transfers, direct deposit, credit cards, travelers' checks and other financial controls and procedures required by a client or production company.

It can get complicated sometimes. Welcome to accounting!

Thankfully, for many of my documentary projects, the budgeting wasn't that terribly difficult. As producer-director-writer I budgeted and estimated my time and rates across the entire project on a two to three page spreadsheet I had created myself. After hiring a small crew at negotiated rates per day or week, I would then consider travel, hotels, meals and vehicles. Calculated equipment costs and tape stock. Then estimated time to edit, editor, music, sound mix, and a final edited master to finish. That was about it, except for a few unique or sundry items along the way (hiring a host or renting a jib). A basic spreadsheet with formulas, categories and totals kept me on budget. I would also update costs as they occurred, so I could track spending and totals.

Without writing a complete book on budgeting, let me tackle just a few of the basics of video, film and documentary categories that you might consider:

TALENT/CREATIVES: Producers, writers, director, actors, talent, director of photography. Your budget and funding - plus their rates - will determine who is paid what. Create deal memos that spell out what services each will perform, for how long and for what rate. Some talent, especially at the top and those well known, often require contracts for their services. Consulting a reputable entertainment lawyer for assistance may be best. Also, consider when the person comes onto the project, for how long, then is finished. A producer may be on the project from first day till last. But a writer's job may be complete after the first day of principle production. You paid for a script, a rewrite, that's it.

CREW: Who you hire - production manager, camera persons, gaffers, grips, audio, production assistants - is based on the nature and size of your project too. Best advice for the crew, as with talent, is to create a straightforward deal memo for as many of the personnel as possible to cut down on any misunderstandings. (Even a clearly worded e-mail will do.) Spell out the days and hours to be worked, rate per day or week, and any other specific costs to be covered, like transportation expenses to the location or per diems for food.

EQUIPMENT: Your shoot could range from a small, single digital camera shoot with basic tripod and lighting kit, to a broadcast HD camera with heavy sticks, to multiple cameras, pedestal tripods, jib and studio lighting. Budget it out, ask around, write down the rates and costs, then calculate and feed the costs into your budget. If renting gear, you can sometimes get a flat weekly rate that will save you production money. Know that when you rent from a reputable equipment house they will either need to setup an account with you (credit checks and bank account info, etc.), need a credit card for a deposit and might need to see a copy of your insurance policy listing them as a covered vendor. You might want to pay extra for their blanket insurance policy to save the time and trouble.

The convenience of working with camera personnel who own equipment is that the hassle of renting can be eliminated by hiring the crew member and their gear as a *complete package*. Come to an understanding about liability if their equipment malfunctions or there is, God forbid, breakage. Talk about that upfront, covering their gear with your insurance when practical. Also, make sure the camera and tape format match your editing scheme and workflow. These days, HD is here to stay. Make sure you choose the right format.

If you have the production funds available, another option is to *purchase your own camera equipment*. But if you are not going to be shooting very many days on your project, or the gear is going back into the box after your short doc or film is complete, it's often smarter simply to rent somebody else's camera.

Spend your money on lighting, sound and a tripod instead. These basic workhorse elements are smarter investments, as good mics and lights hardly go out of style quickly, unlike the latest everyone-is-using-it camera that's the current rage.

TRAVEL: Hotels, meals, transport, out-of-pocket. Keep in mind that the cheapest ticket is not always the best. Two or three stops might mean missed connections or lost luggage. In the long run, late crew or misplaced gear for the shoot cost you far more than you saved. My rule is that the more often you can book non-stops - or no more than a one stop - the better. A good place to stay and tasty meals are critical both for rest and security, plus morale as well. Hotels, meals, transport, etc., are covered later in their own chapter. But travel often can be a big chunk of any production, especially when heading off to various airports for on-location assignments.

INSURANCE/BONDING: This is an area where a production should be wise and careful about scrimping. I once slipped into a moldy pool of water in Bangladesh and dropped a digital camera that was uninsured. The entire production came to a halt, I flew back to Bangkok the next day and lost the rest of my production monies from that client. I was forced to arrange for a replacement camera to be shipped ahead to my next location (Africa), and eventually had to buy a new camera on my return home just to stay in the production game. Insurance matters time and again.

Depending on the size of your project, I would also suggest buying a $1 million liability policy for your production, although that amount doesn't cover what it used to when faced with a lawsuit these days. Such insurance is money well-spent, plus a lot of facilities and vendors require such a policy before you can even setup your lights or walk onto the location or studio.

In the *Travel* chapter I also talk about medical insurance, which is great for both domestic and overseas.

Finally, I've had a lot of experience obtaining a *carnet*, which covers the bonding of your camera and equipment package. A web search under "carnet" will list a number of suppliers. A carnet bond is usually good for twelve months and allows you entrance and exit from more than fifty countries. It is a detailed, itemized document to help facilitate customs clearance in each nation.

PERMITS: Over the course of my career I have had good success with the permit process. Securing approvals *before* you arrive on the scene saves time, confusion, stoppage and money. Permits are worth the fees you pay for them.

When shooting in Paris for *Traveling Lite* years back, we had the great help of the *French Tourism Council*. Our crew shot most everywhere (except on top of the expensive Eiffel Tower) with little or no problems. Shooting permits grease the tracks for good production and, when there is a problem or conflict, can alert the producers, production manager or location scouts early on to potential difficulties ahead.

Contacting the local *film commissioner* (country, state, province, county, city) can be of great value too. These coordinating agencies exist to help you, not hinder you. Plus, their staff may know of other valuable resources and contacts that can often be of great assistance to your project.

Nowhere in my years of shooting have I worked for a more detailed and harder working staff then at CBS's *The Amazing Race*. Our expert team of producers, production managers, researchers and travel coordinators would spend months preparing for twenty-two straight days of difficult global production. Details, logistics, permits, visas, approvals - no one preps like *The Amazing Race*.

Having said that, there is one basic axiom I have used from time to time: "Sometimes it's easier to say you're sorry then to ask for permission." But if you have reasonable funds attached to your project - get shooting permits.

EDITING: With the cost of editing software decreasing dramatically over the years, and the easy availability of laptop computers, the once costly process of editing a video, doc or short film has been streamlined tremendously.

In the linear age you would have to burn window dubs, then edit a rough cut, get approvals, make changes, then correct your edit decision list (EDL). Next step, you'd book an expensive on-line edit suite to create and finish the final master with graphics. Finishing steps were to audio sweeten and mix, lay back, then deliver. Now all of those diverse functions in other locations can be accomplished via non-linear editing on a kitchen table or in the back den. Hurrah!

But even if you are working on a simple one camera project with a small crew, there are still a few basic costs to consider in post. Someone has to pay the editor, who also just might be YOU (unless it's a labor of love with donated time).

You might need to buy a laptop and editing software. Storage - lots of it - is important and very cheap these days. Purchase more than you need. Cabling and renting a playback/record deck might be a factor. Mastering back to the camera is okay for small, short projects, but keep in mind that cameras are primarily for field shooting, not serving as record decks in your edit suite. The wear and tear on the record heads and tape transports only serves a purpose up to a point.

How you ingest/transfer footage, and eventually master, is up to you, your budget and the scope (and professionalism) of your project.

If you are going "out of house" to finalize your project, get in touch with your editor from the very start to confirm how your shooting approach matches the various equipment, systems, software and record/storage formats under their roof.

Other specific post-production elements might come into play too, like adding and buying stock music from a production library, or having a talented friend score a soundtrack for you. Hiring or finding someone capable to do a proper sound mix. (Paying attention to sound is important, as we'll talk about soon.) And thinking through the final output of your project to a digital master, then moving forward to duplication and distribution.

Break down all of these separate elements into their own line items. Consider days in the suite, services rendered and all the little variables to create a solid post-production budget.

Then add a contingency, just in case. Good chance you'll need it.

•

KENYA, EAST AFRICA

Imagine you are standing at the check out desk at the *Intercontinental Hotel* on the edge of busy Nairobi. Your small production crew has just enjoyed three wonderful production days in this colorful East African country. The shoot has gone pretty well, with the recording of key segments and interviews for a very worthy project with a respected faith-based client.

You are the producer-director, and as you pay the final hotel bill you are in total shock. The hotel and meal charges at the *Intercontinental* (plus hefty government taxes) are about three times what you had originally budgeted. In fact, the Kenya location - nine days into a twenty-five day production shoot - has eaten up the entire hotel budget for the rest of the trip. Yet, your team still has numerous ports of call ahead, including South Africa, Brazil, Argentina, plus pinball stops in the USA during the final week.

I can still remember the almost ashen look on the producer's face after paying that sizable Kenya hotel bill. It all came down to the slippery factor of underestimating the mounting cost of a production crew traveling overseas and staying in good, reliable hotels each night. Each day was 3 solid meals, most always in a café or restaurant. Though the other cameraman and I doubled up in the same room, the *Intercontinental* was certainly not cheap. But it was clean, reliable and our "home away from home" for a few important shooting days. Plus, it served as the guardian of our expensive camera, sound and production gear.

Days spent on the road add up. Fast. Anyone worth their salt has underestimated or misjudged a cost or two at some point and been flummoxed when the final bill arrived.

In the producer's case, he adjusted somehow. Not sure what monies he borrowed from what other part of his budget, or how he covered costs during the rest of our trip, but we made it through four more countries, arriving home safe and sound with the recorded tapes safe and secure.

However, that sticker shock on his face in Nairobi is still etched on my mind years later.

•

PICK TWO

It is not uncommon for productions to sometimes miscalculate or underestimate what a project will eventually cost. In fact, some shoots have serious budget problems and funding before their very first image is even recorded. Even for a major studio film. But when it comes to video, docs and short films, there is an old adage I heard years back that seems truly appropriate:

Good. Fast. Cheap. Pick two.

In my career, I have witnessed two types of clients: those who go cheap, and those who endeavor to do it right.

The "do it right" client usually understands through experience, dedication and vision what it will cost to produce a project that hits the mark creatively, artistically and technically. Their production money repeatedly ends up on the screen.

The "cheap" client, however, attempts from the outset - or at various stops along the way - to save every last dime, to maximize their profit or conserve their limited funds. By going cheap, they are diluting the production quality, and also signaling to talent, staff and crew that the goal is cheap, not good.

I understand that few productions can write blank checks, or that a lot of budgets get squeezed due to unforeseen circumstances. We've all been there. And most any reputable producer, production manager or staff accountant at some point has attempted financially to spin gold out of a pile of straw.

Just make sure you are funded properly and budgeted correctly before hitting the GO switch for production.

Be very careful where and how you scrimp.

•

BUDGET TACTICS FROM PROS

"Get the money upfront!"

- Rick Eisleben, director-cameraman

"One time we needed a shot of our main character on a bus. Instead of renting a bus, we bought three bus tickets!"

- Donna L. Turner, Horizon Gate Productions

"Have a 5-10% buffer for unexpected costs if possible."

- Steve Taylor, Digital Spatula

"Budget: no matter how small or large the project is - have a budget. If you don't know how to create one it's worth it to spend a little money and hire someone with experience to create one with you and for you. Once you have a budget don't get too locked into set amounts for things, be willing to shift money around as needed, as long as you don't go over that bottom line you established.

"Realize that sometimes it's better to spend a little more money in one area knowing it will bring costs down overall, rather than pinching those pennies too hard.

"If you get production elements donated - locations, props, equipment, etc. - be sure to track what those items would have cost you so that you have an idea of what your budget actually would have been if you'd paid for them - good info for the next project!"

- Mary-Pat Carney, World Race Productions

"When you're working on no or low budget, there has to be a capacity to pre-visualize at a very high level. If the director does not have this gift, he should surround himself with those who do. This gift results in a flexibility and confidence that spreads through the crew like a wildfire. And it will save you a truckload of money.

"The usual mantra is...Cutting out all that is unnecessary at the script stage saves you 100% of your budget. Cutting out all that is unnecessary in the pre-production stage saves you 20%. Cutting out all that is unnecessary in production save you 5%.

"And making these cuts in the editing room is a disaster!"

- Bart Gavigan, Spark Productions

"Some 'non creative' things to think about...

"Create an LLC (vs. DBA) and get a reseller's permit.

"Get general liability insurance ($1-$2 million minimum).

"Get signed release forms and either SS/EIN numbers from everyone: crew, talent, etc. (paid and non-paid).

"Get signed release forms for all source materials (photos, video, etc.) from everyone who provides it for your production.

"Always try to negotiate "in perpetuity" for all services and materials (voice-over, music libraries, stock footage, etc.).

"Never, ever use any type of non-cleared copyrighted material (corporate logos, clothing with logos, wall posters that appear in shots, music being played in the background, etc.)."

-Bruce R. Bennett, executive producer, Creative Inspiration

CHAPTER 7 REVIEW: BUDGET

1. People, vendors, services and facilities have to be paid for.
2. Manage your production money wisely.
3. Find (and use) budgeting software to track costs.
4. How you estimate and track your budget is incredibly important to the very lifeline of prep and production. Budget also impacts post-production workflow, timelines and delivery.
5. Contacting the local film commissioner (country, state, province, county, city) can be of great value.
6. No two film or video shoots are exactly alike.
7. Be very careful where and how you scrimp.
8. Good. Fast. Cheap. Pick two.

CHAPTER 8: CLIENTS & TALENT

Movers & Shakers

•

"When the elephants fight, the grass gets trampled."

- African proverb

CLIENTS

Over the years I have been privileged to work with both notable clients...and the very obscure. It's been an eclectic range of leading networks, agencies and production companies all the way down to the small business, group or charity that wants a documentary or promo segment created to tell their story or sell their product well.

There have been difficult clients, and those so professional and sincere that I would gladly walk over hot coals to produce projects with them again.

I've had clients who advanced production monies upfront on the quick to get the ball rolling, and those I had to chase for months to get the final payment. But, of course, they demanded the show master *immediately* upon completion.

There have been many clients who honored our contract, and those who were constantly working around the rough edges to skirt our agreement and benefit their cash flow...or get the final product.

I've had numerous clients who were brilliant in early meetings but got "chippy" near the end. There were those who really didn't know what they wanted until we had shot, edited and had shown the completed project to them...*then* came the endless round of changes to script, music, narration and editing.

Where to start?

I've begun to believe that rather than clients asking for our references we, perhaps, should ask them for *theirs*. I am not kidding. If you are an independent contractor (freelance, DBA doing business as, LLC or an INC) you need to know better who you are about to go into business with. If they are somewhat new to production, or have limited knowledge of media with its potential and power, then it is your responsibility to lead them by the hand.

However, if you are working on an already established show or series, there is probably a production company culture that's already been established. Find out what that culture is as soon as possible. Ask around. Get some feedback. What is the reputation of the producers shooting that show? Even the production assistant or the receptionist has an opinion that will give you a clearer picture of just how things are typically run. You need to know.

I will say this: **most clients are good people trying hard to realize their goal, whether it's a commercial, video, film, TV show or documentary**.

•

SPRINGFIELD, MO

One simple, but extremely important phone call early in my film career changed everything for me. It was a January '86 conversation involving Ed Nelson, who headed up the missions communication department of a leading Protestant church denomination, *The Assemblies of God*, headquartered in Missouri.

I had just completed for this group a very successful video project shot on-location in Thailand. It was a milestone video that truly established to Ed - and the A/G - that I could hit the benchmark when it came to quality production and storytelling. The Thailand video was a labor of love that I put countless hours into editing - and it showed.

My call to Ed was an exploratory venture to see if perhaps his group wanted to produce more videos like what we had recently produced in Thailand. Hesitantly, I asked Ed on the phone, "do you want to do more?" He paused for what seemed like an eternity before answering, "yes, I'd like to do six."

His answer floored me. Six videos would mean my venturing out on my own without the shelter of working for the large humanitarian group where I was, at that time, employed as a documentary filmmaker. Thailand had been shot previously during one of my vacations. But six videos for a new series, in my estimation, would take at least two years to complete. This would be a big, challenging project - more than just two weeks of vacation time might handle.

Over the course of another ten to fifteen minutes of conversation with Ed we sketched out what would become the *Unreached People* video series. It would become a multi-episode exploration of spiritual beliefs across the world. And those six videos would eventually morph into 13 twenty minute documentaries shot across four years (traveling to 44 countries).

What Ed expertly provided from the very inception of the *Unreached People* video series was what most every filmmaker or video producer would want from most any important client.

First, Ed had a specific vision as to *exactly* what he wanted the video series to explore and say. And he was able to articulate that vision expertly, and clearly, through numerous conversations, meetings and memos.

To our project's benefit, Ed was always extremely easy and pleasant to work with. He was smart, funny, articulate, secure and a great listener. Ed had complete trust in my new little production company - and me. He believed that I would bring my hard earned expertise to the endeavor, plus crew, gear, effort and ingenuity.

Ed was never in any true hurry and was possessed with immense patience, realizing that it would take a number of global production trips just to gather footage and interviews before we'd ever even see the light of day with the first video. This turned out to be four major overseas trips, and a year's worth of planning and shooting, before video #1 (Western Europe) was scripted, edited and finished.

In addition, Ed provided tremendous resources, both Stateside and globally. We had a very workable budget, and our team was always paid in a timely manner. Never did we have to check on an invoice or wonder when the next payment was going to arrive.

Further, Ed supplied contacts and resources across the world who were tied to his group through association. Wherever we went as a camera crew, there were A/G staff and people on the ground ready to assist. They setup interviews, drove us to locations and provided information and insight to our project. We had a bounty of riches - people, transport and materiel - when it came to ground support.

Years later, I can't think of any conflict or skirmish Ed and I ever had on any issue, large or small. The easy flow of respect, trust and communication between us was ideal. And when there was a conflict in the field, Ed would fix it personally - by phone, fax or letter. This included politics, which sometimes reared its ugly head as we moved through other people's territories and hemispheres of influence.

In all our travels, Ed never once accompanied us. Nor did he want copious reports. Just an update from time to time. Ed was only "hands on" when it was truly necessary, usually during the planning, scripting and editing phases. He'd fine-tune a point, or change a word here and there. Ed might select another shot or make a wise suggestion after seeing the rough cut. Nine times out of ten, his feedback made the sequence stronger, better or more inspirational.

Strategically, Ed could see six to twelve months ahead in the timeline as to our future locations and travel. During our two to three meetings each year, we'd map out countries and assignments far ahead so as to take advantage of ideal weather and local conditions. That way we rarely shot during rainy, hot or cold seasons, meaning that we almost always arrived in a nation or region during the very best possible shooting environments. This paid off time and again in great working conditions and favorable weather.

Ed Nelson was the absolute best client I have ever worked with throughout my entire career. Ed "got it." He thoroughly understood the true power and potential of media and video. He was also a great learner, able to soak-up production concepts as we explained them.

In the end, Ed spoiled me, for he was the perfect client most of us wished we worked for *all* of the time. And to his answering, "Yes, I'd like to do six videos," I will forever be indebted.

Thanks, Ed. You were (and are) the best.

CLIENTS ARE VITAL

All of us in the production world will work with and for a client at some point in our careers. Unless you are entirely self-funded, it's inevitable that your talents will be engaged by a client on a project. Even if you've raised the money and shot your dream documentary, you will have to eventually deal with film festival directors or distribution representatives or television executives. They constitute "clients" too. And it's important for you to understand where these many types of clients are coming from at the very start, if at all practical and possible.

If they are a *film festival*, then they want your project to fit into their programming mix. They may have hundreds or thousands of submissions. If you make the final cut, congratulations on being part of their fest. But talk through premieres, showings and publicity too.

Should you be dealing with d*istribution or licensing*, then you might want to engage the services of a reputable entertainment lawyer - or an agent. Ask around, get references and referrals. A good lawyer or agent should be working for YOU, not themselves.

If you are shooting for an *ad agency*, they will have certain expectations. Which include professionalism in your approach to market their own client's services or a specific product. You will encounter creative directors and account reps that are VERY active in how the spot, segment or commercial is to be shot, produced, edited and articulated. My only suggestion is to try to get onto the same page from the very start. Talk about role definitions clearly. And keep the lines of communication open so conflicts can be resolved smoothly with progress made.

Should your client be a *corporation, company, foundation, non-profit, charity or organization*...it will be important to know how the project you're working on will be used, what the theme and message is, who the audience will be and how important the project is overall. Make sure to create a contract or deal memo, and be specific about all the details of who does what, the budget and payment terms, the shooting schedule, approvals, delivery and finalizing. Talk this all through at the very beginning.

Sometimes one will be working as a freelancer for another production company that already has a project in place, with budgets set and a timeline scheduled for shooting and editing. Often you will complete a W-9 form and will create invoices for the specific services you've performed.

If you have been hired by this company before, and have an already established relationship, then you will be working with a certain familiarity. But if you are new to the production company, then ask, listen and learn what their expectations are from the start. When does overtime kick in? Is this an eight hour day or ten? What type of shoot are we doing? Anything special or unique about the client, shoot or show? These questions will help you to better understand role definitions and production conditions. After a few shoots, you will get the hang of how a project is being shot and what the leaders expect.

In the end, certain clients can be very demanding, and sometimes terribly difficult. If they are demanding, there is usually a reason. Find out what that is and how it affects your job or responsibility - and the project.

Should they be difficult, it is your choice as to whether you want to continue working with and for them. Are they being unreasonable? Unrealistic? If so, why - or why not? It's your call. If their behavior lapses into a hostile work environment, abuse or sexual harassment (and this does happen) then you have certain rights. Exercise them.

If there is conflict, try to resolve it quickly. Usually, if tensions fester, there is wailing and gnashing of teeth as the project concludes. Talk to each other sooner rather than later, put the pointed fingers down and try very hard to keep feelings calm and collected. That's why *post mortems* are valuable: By meeting frequently, hardly a day goes by where issues large and small aren't addressed and rectified.

In the end, know that the vast majority of clients - large and small - are wonderful, great, talented people whose primary goals are to accomplish media projects that are truly special and significant.

Help them achieve their goals, and they'll hire you time and again.

TALENT

It's been my privilege to work with some very famous people in my career. Singers, rock stars, actors, athletes. Time and again, they were absolutely great to work with and provided solid interviews or stand up hosting. They made the shoot go smoother and faster - and more professional. And they had wonderful stories to tell off-camera.

The only times I have ever had difficulties with a "star" is when working with those who one might consider to be minor celebrities, performers who had once been on a sitcom or who played roles in smaller pictures. Or whose star had faded long ago. The feeling was that they thought they were far more important than they really were. Their demands and attitude (and those of their agent) could be truly embarrassing sometimes. But those occasions have been, thankfully, few and far between.

The beauty of working with professionals is that they can often bring life to your script, while knocking out their lines in just a few takes. They are able to walk, talk and hit their mark consistently. That's why they do what they do well - they're incredibly good at it. And those years, or decades, of experience show in the final product.

Stars bring something extra to the screen that amateurs rarely can.

Beyond stars, there are three other types of talent this chapter must talk about, or this book would be remiss in handling the aspect of talent: **presenters, actors and narrators**.

If you have a dramatic script that requires acting, **choose the best actors you can find**. If someone is right and natural for the part, but more expensive than your budget can afford, try very hard to still secure their services. Find room in your budget if at all possible.

*A **good** actor will make an average script much better. And a **great** actor will elevate a good script to new heights. Their efforts will show on-screen.*

On-camera presenters are equally important too. For they set the tone and mood - while providing information - of your piece. Try to cast presenters that do hosting for a living. Handsome and beautiful are fine. But professional and natural are better.

Sometimes a client will want to use the local newscaster or a minor talent who is popular in your town or region. Or a distant relative that their spouse likes. They will pressure you. But it's far more important to find someone that's appropriate for the role you have written, and who is completely professional in their presentation.

Don't skimp on finding the best person for on-camera duties. They are up there on your screen telling your story. Sometimes you will luck out and can engage the services of a well known actor who believes in your cause. Treat them well, for they are doing you and your project a huge favor.

In the end, find the very best presenter you can.

Finally, I believe that **excellent narrators (voice-overs) are worth their weight in gold.** Sure, they charge strong fees many times for their services. But they can and will bring life to your script just through their reading, intonation and delivery.

I have had tremendous success with voice-overs through the years. And 99% of them are absolute sweethearts to work with. These days, many of them work alone in faraway studios...so you never actually see them. But their voices are the performance you will cut your picture to for the final product.

My only suggestions in working with narrators are these:

First, make sure you have the *right voice* for your script. Listen to some demo cd's or web links presenting their skills, narrowing the field to those you think are appropriate. Have a casting agent do some demos with these voices, having them read a single script page.

Second, once you've chosen the right voice-over, *be specific with that person as to what you're looking for*. Tell them if this is a high energy promo, a wildlife documentary or an exploration into political corruption. Each genre requires a different type of read, performance and approach.

Next, make sure the *client and producers sign-off on the final voice chosen.* In the past I have had to change voice-overs after the fact because the client didn't like the narrator chosen after all, even though I thought the person was ideal. Make sure everyone likes the voice.

In addition, *make sure your script is complete before you go to record.* Each time you come back to the narrator with script changes, there is a new, extra fee to pay. Finish script, then record.

Finally, *don't wear your narrator out.* You don't need to do twenty-seven takes of a single paragraph when your instinct told you take four was the keeper. Sure, maybe do a safety take. But going past ten takes and on to infinity only shows your indecision. With proper direction and feedback, most professional narrators can nail a great read within three to four takes. And if you have a long script, countless takes means you'll be recording forever. That's when fatigue and frustration sets in.

Actors, presenters and narrators are valuable on and off screen creative assets to your project. Find the right person for the part, then let them bring your words and pictures to life.

Here's a great final tip when working with people who are in front of the camera: *Treat normal people like CELEBRITIES. And treat celebrities like NORMAL people.*

•

SAN FRANCISCO, CA

Okay, since it's my book, I get to name drop at least once.

The nicest, easiest and most professional person I've *ever* worked with on-camera was Tony Bennett, the legendary jazz singer.

Working for ABC Network's *In Concert* late night music series, it was my total joy and privilege to interview Mr. Bennett as he was pitching a new CD he had recorded featuring the songs of the late, legendary actor-dancer, Fred Astaire.

The venue was the majestic *Fairmont Hotel* in San Francisco. Our crew had setup in a side part of the massive lobby. As director, I was told which suite Mr. Bennett was staying in, and about fifteen minutes before we were to shoot I knocked on his door. He opened, said hi, and I introduced myself. Ready to go, he locked the door and we walked to the elevator making small talk as we went.

Down through the grand lobby we went, and the people who instantly recognized Mr. Bennett as he walked through the corridor to our setup parted like Moses dividing the Red Sea. To each person who said hi to him, Mr. Bennett was unfailingly polite. Big smile, smooth voice, how you doing, sweet as can be.

We sat down, got him miked up, adjusted lights a bit, and I told him a few of the interview ground rules. All of which he thought were more than fine. And off we went for the next thirty minutes talking to one of the most famous singers in the world.

Mr. Bennett could not have been nicer or easier to work with. What you saw was exactly what you got. Tony Bennett was as cool and classy as can be. And unpretentious. I'd throw him questions about the new album, and he'd give a great sound bite or two. Ask him to make an observation about Astaire, and he'd speak about the late performer's dedicated attention to detail and rehearsal. All of Bennett's on-camera responses ended-up being great material for the final broadcast segment. And then we were done.

Never have I worked with such a wonderful professional with so few demands or attitude. Tony was Tony. Easy as pie.

May they all grow up to be Tony Bennett someday.

•

CLIENT/TALENT TACTICS FROM PROS

"When dealing with actors (well-known or not), interviewees, guests, etc. never assume familiarity. It's ALWAYS 'yes sir' and 'yes ma'am' until/unless you're told otherwise."

- Charley Buchanan, PBS cameraman

"Years ago, I directed a short film for a commercial client from Asia. We shot in Canada because they didn't want to pay union fees, and were under the gun because of the client's schedule. As a result, they pressured me to select actors that I didn't personally believe in, and were under-qualified for the roles. It was the worst experience I've ever had, and a huge strategic and creative error.

"In planning a production, few issues are more important than talent. No matter how great your script or how brilliant your directing, without a great actor or spokesperson to pull it off, you're doomed. The single greatest mistake young filmmakers and video producers make is skimping on talent. Don't do it. Invest. Take the time. Find the right people. You'll never regret it.

"One of the things I learned early is the power of saying 'no.'

"I directed a music video here in Los Angeles with an artist who at the time was a major performer on Broadway. It was an elaborate video shot on a huge set. The video would be broadcast globally the evening of New Year 2000 to celebrate the new millennium. But from the moment we signed the deal with the performer, his agent became a major pain. He didn't like the studio we selected. He didn't like the schedule. He didn't like the style of the video. He didn't like anything we came up with. I tried and tried to be nice and accommodating, but nothing worked.

"Finally, a week before shooting, the agent called and was upset about something new. In desperation, I blurted out: 'Look. Obviously, you're not happy with the shoot, the project, my decisions, or anything else. And if you're not happy, your star client won't be happy. So why don't we just pull the plug and call it quits right now? I think it would be best for everyone.' There was an awkward moment of silence, and then the agent completely changed. 'Oh, no, no, no. You didn't understand,' he begged. 'I was just trying to be helpful.' From that point on, he became a teddy bear. He was encouraging, supportive, and on the day of the shoot spent most of the day getting me coffee.

"That's the project where I learned that until you're ready to say 'no,' your 'yes' means nothing. Never underestimate the power of walking away. Don't overuse it, but when it's necessary, you have to be ready to say NO. Once you learn that, it will change everything."

- Phil Cooke, award-winning film/tv director

"I remember early on when we would have to interview a celebrity, I would get star struck. (Who am I kidding? I still get star struck!) Here are a couple of quick tips:

"Focus on the project, not the star. Too many people (myself included) get side-tracked by celebrity. By consciously focusing all attention on what's best for the project, you'll seem less nervous, and probably put the star at ease.

"Don't let 'fandom' take over! Save the autographs, pictures, etc. for after the shoot, if at all. Too many young filmmakers go overboard with how big of a fan they are, and it can be off-putting to the celebrity.

"Remember, they're people, just like you. They want the project to be good, just like you. As long as your courteous, professional, and don't show how star struck you are, you'll be just fine."

- Biagio Messina, Joke Productions

"Big shots never walk alone...they are usually accompanied by aides."

- Bob Sheiffer, CBS News

"Never take pictures of or with stars on a set while you are on duty - it's totally tacky and completely unprofessional. The set is supposed to be a place where they can hide from paparazzi and do their job without the feeling of being 'stalked'. I'm sure there are exceptions, but people sneaking pics/videos and posting them on *YouTube* or *TMZ* is just stupid!"

- Steve Thiel, freelance cameraman

"It is never a client's responsibility to ask you, to tell you or to understand anything about [film, television or media]. It is YOUR responsibility to educate them."

- Dr. Marty Cohen, Cohen-Brown Picture Company

"Just a tip: Consider multiplying the distribution of your documentary by doing different language versions. Beware of poor conventional translations and always look for a good adaptation of the script to other languages.

"Last, but not least, you should think about finding the right voices for the narration and voice-overs, this is applicable for all language versions, including the original. Focusing so much on the picture side, some documentarians don't pay attention to music and specially voice delivery. Getting the right voices will contribute greatly to the doc's success."

- Constantino de Miguel, recording studio owner

CHAPTER 8 REVIEW: CLIENTS & TALENT

1. Most clients are good people trying hard to realize their goal, whether it's a commercial, video, film, TV show or documentary.
2. Choose the best actors you can find.
3. A *good* actor will make an average script much better. And a *great* actor will elevate a good script to new heights. Their efforts will show on-screen.
4. Don't skimp on finding the best person(s) for on-camera duties.
5. Excellent narrators (voice-overs) are worth their weight in gold.

CHAPTER 9: COLLEAGUES & CREW

Picking the Right Team

•

"I'm not under too much of an illusion of how smart or un-smart I am - because filmmaking ultimately is about teamwork."

- Guy Ritchie, film director

The right team of people on your project is extremely critical to its very success.

Production is rarely created in a vacuum. There are few one man or woman bands, though they exist sometimes. The only person I've ever heard of that could "do it all" was Stevie Wonder, who played every instrument and sang all his songs for one of his records. But despite Stevie's considerable talents and skills, he still required a recording engineer to set the levels and master the tapes. He also depended on a studio assistant to place the mics, run the cables and setup the stands. Despite his fingerprint all over his record, he did require help.

Filmmaking (production) by its very nature is a collaborative process. Most everyone must hire, engage and depend on other team members to accomplish certain defined tasks within the overall project. That includes writers, directors, producers, production assistants, music composers, makeup artists, editors, gaffers, lighting directors, videotape op's, videographers, grips, truck drivers...the list goes on.

Repeatedly, I like to hire talented, experienced people that are far better at their crafts than I am.

My skills in camerawork are pretty good, but I often engage the services of others who are many notches above my shooting ability. That way, as the director, I don't have to worry about the shots or framing as much, just the interview or performance. And a good cameraperson will make framing or technical suggestions, which bring quality and creativity to the shoot.

My lighting skills are good - but on any shoot larger than a basic interview, I usually hire a professional DP. The segment will look far better for it, and DP's know various little tricks with lighting and cosmetics that would never have occurred to me.

Hiring people who are better than you at their crafts is a sure sign of security and confidence. Giving them credit where it is due shows unselfishness and grace, too.

On many projects, I first rough cut my interviews, categorize my best visuals and then organize my best sound bites on *Final Cut Pro*. But after working out a basic timeline and moving a few segments around into a possible sequence or two, I then book a skilled editor to come in and start taking these raw ingredients to turn them into an even better, more polished project. It's like baking a cake: I'll gather the main ingredients, but it's the editor who helps me bake the cake and put the final icing on - little squiggly decorations and all.

A good colleague, Jeff Callaway, is a far superior sound man than I am, having been nominated for 5 *Emmys* for his work on *COPS* and *The Rockford Files*. So he is present at many of my shoots, bringing his own portable sound mixer, cables and connectors. He makes sure everything is patched correctly, while watching the audio levels with intent. Jeff worries about the wireless transmitters, the fish pole, zep and the lavaliere mics. I hardly worry about audio, Jeff does.

In the grand scheme of things, using talented people should never be considered a luxury or rarity, but a basic necessity.

Yes, talented, creative and technical people come with day rates, and many of them are rarely cheap to hire. But they are there to collaborate with you directly and professionally, to enhance your quality and vision, no matter the project's form or intent.

A few words about everyone just getting along: it's desired, but not absolutely required, especially if you are booking a large crew. Sometimes a little tension can actually be good, for it drives the engine of focus and dedication. Just try to keep the lines of communication open, resolving conflict whenever possible.

But as long as everyone is doing their job professionally and capably, don't sweat the little skirmishes.

In my case, my experience overseas (and with virtually any location production) has also taught me to gravitate mostly to people with both artistic sensibilities and a good, healthy sense of humor. (A little laughter is like good medicine.) There is, naturally, a time to be serious, and a time to laugh (as long as the humor or jokes are not malicious, insensitive or demeaning).

People who have travelled extensively, are superb at what they do and are funny too are usually great to work with. I have found they will often have a good mix of the sensitivity to get you through that tough shoot in Nairobi's poverty stricken Mithari Valley, and the soft humor to lighten the mood later that night over dinner at the local hotel.

Be aware that insensitivity and cynicism can ruin almost any shoot or project. And truly toxic people, those who are constantly complaining from sun up till sun down, will poison the communal waters for everyone involved. Don't hire team and crew members who are chronically negative.

My point? Try whenever you can to hire experienced, talented, good humored team who will join you in creating good shoots and can tackle your projects with skill, dedication and effort. That's for on the road, in the studio, at the airline gate, inside the production office or in the edit bay.

When you pick a great team, with the right people doing the right jobs, everyone wins.

•

TOKYO, JAPAN

One of the most difficult and troubling projects I have ever worked on in my career was for a major corporate video shot in Tokyo, Japan in the early 90s. The client was a nationally respected media production company who had highly recommended me to another producer within their group. She contacted me about a possible shoot in Tokyo, asked about prices and dates, then I put the camera package together, along with the crew. My supporting role was to serve as both a production manager and sound/lighting tech. The producer was West Coast, the director East Coast.

Various team members and clients were arriving into Tokyo separately on the same day, but we had all coordinated our trans-Pacific airplane flights to arrive within a few minutes of each other. Meeting up in customs at Narita Airport, I met my new clients for the first time, then began filling out the required carnet forms for our equipment clearance into Japan. But the customs official assisting me spoke English that was a bit difficult to understand at times, so I misunderstood a few questions or suggestions he asked now and then, till everything was finally sorted out.

To my new clients standing nearby, my misunderstanding a few phrases somehow represented a sense of incompetence on my part. Despite my long resumé of overseas production and travel, the awkwardness of clearing customs seemed to raise some nagging doubts with the producer and director. So, they made some snide comments on the spot that I could hear. We were already getting off to a rough start.

The next day in Tokyo, our crew had lunch at the sponsoring company's downtown office, joined by a few Japanese colleagues. Eating together was to give our team more time during the introductory process to talk over the script and schedule for the week. At one point during the bento box meal, I added soy sauce to my white rice, and got a quizzical look from a few Japanese people at the table. Somehow I had committed a minor faux pas with the soy. Later, I was reprimanded a few times by the producer and the director of the "big", incredibly stupid cultural mistake I was judged to have made - as if my rice fiasco had brought terrible shame on their leadership, the company and the production.

During the actual shoots, I was not only setting up sound and cables, but assisting with lighting too, running plugs and cords into various rooms. The director walking around during our first setup quickly criticized me for not taping down light cables fast enough with gaffer tape. This came at a point when the lighting positions hadn't even been decided on yet. It didn't seem to matter to him that lights weren't set, or to understand that I was working as fast and as diligently as possible, actually charged with doing two jobs at once. I was being sniped at again; Criticism abounded.

At one point, in a packed conference room, an extra piece of video equipment was being considered for possible rental for the upcoming production week, perhaps another monitor for client viewing. But the item seemed important to the powers that be. I was asked directly if getting that piece of gear by the next morning in vast Tokyo was possible. Put on the spot, I mentioned I would certainly check around, and offered that the piece of gear would probably be an extra cost to the shoot. That turned out to be a big mistake.

After the pre-production meeting was over, while we were walking back to our vehicles, the producer walked up next to me and, under her breath, chastised me very sternly with, "don't you ever discuss costs and money in front of my clients like that ever again!!! Do you understand me?!" Then walked away.

Left stunned, I began wondering just what wave lengths or frequency we were all now transmitting on - Morse code? Were we now producing reality show segments? I had just been scolded for something not even aware I'd done wrong. My position was that I was being asked how quickly to find and rent a new, unanticipated piece of gear in an unfamiliar city. Forgive me, but since no one had gone over the ground rules, I was wondering if budget was an issue on this project, which is why I brought it up. But this obviously had embarrassed and irked the producer, who decided to let me know her intense displeasure pronto.

In the mind of the producer, my bringing up rental for the gear in a crowded room of clients and colleagues was like striking up a lit match at an ammunition dump.

A few days later, at coffee or some other innocent moment, the producer apologized and explained - and rationalized - her heated words to me. She ratcheted down her anger. But the serious damage was already done. I didn't like these people, nor did I want to work with them.

This once exotic Japanese corporate video shoot was turning into a minor disaster, at least for the lighting/sound tech - me. My fitting into this quickly assembled team was like forcing a round peg into a square hole. Someone get me off this shoot.

If I could have left the country without facing a lawsuit, and didn't need the money, I would have packed my camera gear immediately, headed out to Narita Airport and caught the very next flight home to the States. But I couldn't. I had to finish the shoot, and was required to by contract. No matter how terrible I felt about the working conditions, I had to stick it out.

Miscommunication and suspicion were poisoning my working relationship with the overly critical producer and director, who were forever convinced I was somehow a bumbling idiot. Working on a shoot in a faraway nation where you are treated rudely and viewed with hostility - where most every word you say or tiny action you take is criticized - becomes deplorable...and miserable.

I was stuck with this sniping leadership team, with no convenient way of getting out of town, literally.

So I counted the days till we were to finish and leave Japan. In the meantime, I grew quiet, saying little or nothing. My new survival tactic was to keep my head down and stay to my own ways, doing my job as efficiently as I could, but go unnoticed when I could. My only solace was that I had befriended one of the clients on the Japan team, so I would gravitate to that person when eating or traveling together.

Finally, and mercifully, the last day arrived, and we said our stock goodbyes at the airport nervously. But I'm sure my good reputation would take an unfair hit once the producer and director got back home and did their own versions of a *post mortem* when asked how their exotic shoot in Japan had gone. My services were never called on again by that production company. Fine. It happens.

If I had to do it all over again, I would have asked the producer and director - as professionally as possible - to let me do my job, to knock it off and to get off my back. Request that they tell me just what the proper ground rules there were for their project. Try to straighten the fragmented lines of expectations. Funny how some pushy people will back down when you standup to them. But I was younger then, trying hard not to rock the boat, to be nice. Chalk it up to experience. What do they call it these days - *a teaching moment*?

In the end, what I learned from the tenuous Japan assignment was that some teams are destined to fail based on style and personality differences. Sometimes, it's just not meant to be. As you gain experience, you'll come to realize that it's impossible to keep every single client and producer happy *all the time* on every shoot. If you please around seven out of ten clients, producers, agency people and other hierarchy, your average is pretty decent.

But the Japan shoot taught me to be very cautious and careful about what you say in a packed conference room, even when put on the spot.

And to never, never, ever pour soy sauce on your rice.

•

FREELANCE

One of the great benefits of working and hiring within the freelance world is that if a person (an independent contractor) doesn't work out on a specific shoot, you are rarely obligated to go back to that person again. A one day production doesn't mean you're committed for life to work together. The process is more like a *first date* to see if and how it all works out.

Should the shoot not go well, you can go your separate ways and just move on, no feelings hurt. If the project and experience was enjoyable, then you might swap cell numbers, e-mail addresses and business cards. Hey, let's do this again. Over time, you may work on a number of shoots, sometimes over many years. I have colleagues I've known and worked with for 20+ years. I am ready, willing and able to jump on an airplane with them on a moment's notice.

Should you be in a position to hire support staff for a project or to crew a shoot, it's best to do a little homework first. Ask around, calling other crew, clients or contacts who've worked with a prospective crew or production person before. If the candidate has references listed on their resumé with phone numbers or e-mail addresses, contact them. Get recommendations if possible, no matter what role they might play - producer, grip, production assistant or editor.

Ask, what's the person like? Are they good at what they do? A hard worker? How about personality - easy to get along with? Difficult? Moody? Profane? Solid and dependable?

If the person has built up a sizable list of credits for a number of notable clients, then something must be going right for them. Otherwise, they wouldn't be staying busy and booked. That may not always be the case every time, but is true most of the time.

Try to take a look at a work sample or clip, or go to their website. Call and talk to them on the phone. Try to setup a meeting at a coffee house or at your place of business. Whatever is appropriate that helps you learn their background, talents and to get a sense of their abilities.

It is a fundamental principle that people usually like to hire those colleagues they've worked with before. It's a familiarity factor: we usually go with those we know. That's been my case too. If a shoot comes my way as a producer or director, I am more than likely to call someone already in my rolodex or contact list before calling an unknown quantity. I am quicker to trust someone I've walked through the fire with rather than a person out-of-the-blue.

The legendary executive producer of *The Amazing Race*, Bert van Munster, relies on many of the same battle-tested crew members he's worked with after many seasons and scores of countries. 90% of the crew have worked with Bert before at some point, a few since the very inception of the series. (That's true for a number of show's producers too.)

Bert, through his extensive travels, has collected his own professional roster of cameramen, sound men plus tech and logistical support personnel along the way. The production crew are drawn from across the world, not just the USA. They come from Israel, South Africa, Canada, the UK, Brazil and throughout Europe. Their sometimes faraway locations are irrelevant for such a massive, globally-based series. *The Amazing Race* crew roster is extremely reliable, in great shape and delivers the goods time and again. These team members are some of the hardest working shooters and audio guys (twenty hour days sometimes) you will find anywhere at anytime. Bert goes with what he knows and can depend on; he is rarely disappointed.

If you are new or up-and-coming, becoming a key contact in someone's rolodex or on a crew roster is important. You want your phone to ring, an e-mail to arrive or a text message to come in asking if you have an open date and are available. That comes down to a) Being really good at what you do. b) Networking and keeping in contact with possible colleagues. c) Continuing to deliver an excellent attitude and work ethic - plus creative, technical or artistic abilities that are in demand and valuable.

Being a great, likable person also helps. Reliability is a huge asset too.

•

HAVANA, CUBA

Having someone dedicated and reliable to assist you on-site in another country, region, province, state or county that is foreign to you is absolutely essential.

A good production coordinator, location scout, guide, translator, driver or production assistant - all are an important, temporary part of the team too. Their knowledge, skills and abilities can contribute to your success, or failure. Without help on the ground, you will, instead, be wandering alone, figuring everything out on your own while losing precious, valuable time trying to navigate among unfamiliar roads, peoples, cultures, languages and locations.

One such valuable person who helped me expertly in the past in Cuba is a location manager named Belkis. (I have omitted her last name for security sake.) Without her help, I'm sure I'd have landed in a dark, filthy prison or been escorted out of the country immediately.

Of all the countries I have directed and shot in, Cuba remains at the top of a very short list as the most paranoid. Everyone seems to be spying on everyone else. Casual conversations are overheard at restaurants. Mail is opened, read, resealed. Streets are watched and names remembered. There is a clandestine level of communication that goes on throughout this sealed off Caribbean island due to their power and fear of Fidel Castro, and now his brother, Raul, too.

Visually, Havana is one of the most beautiful "beat-up" cities in the world. The buildings have weathered terribly in the hot tropical sun and constant rain. Nothing gets fixed or painted properly. This faded, unfinished presentation gives this worn capital a look like no other. Tattered and torn, Havana is loaded with texture and detail, possessing a faded, picturesque glory.

Years back, I setup an assignment to Cuba to cover their famous sex industry for the TV series *Investigative Reports*, hosted by the respected, legendary television anchor, Bill Kurtis. I landed in Havana via a side country, carrying a separate Cuban entry visa, but without possessing a valid shooting permit. (As if Fidel would have approved my subject to begin with.)

Through the interwoven grapevine of television producers and managers, Belkis had become well known as a "fixer." She could arrange for most everything you basically needed as a TV crew to do your shoot properly, even if staying under the radar of Cuban officials and their secret police was necessary. From location scouting to transportation to translation, Belkis knew Havana like the back of her beautiful, brown Latina hand. And she was truly wonderful to be around - pleasant, good-natured and with a sweet sense of humor. She also knew the best places to eat, shop and sight see.

For a segment so potentially dangerous, the great thing about working with Belkis was that she also understood, after many location shoots with outside crews, the unique nature and requirements of television, especially that a camera team wants to use their time wisely and productively. There was no mañana with her. She had already arranged a car with a driver for my time, and had surveyed some key locations. Belkis knew, through experience, where I could shoot numerous late night interviews with "jineteras" (working girls) clandestinely, and how to setup my camera near dance clubs and hotels packed with tourists where the girls plied their trade.

Looking back over our few days in Havana doing a risky, undercover shoot, I now realize just how valuable Belkis was in keeping me truly safe and sound. Her expert coordinating and "fixing" led to some good footage used during the award-winning *Red Light Districts* TV special.

I'd work with Belkis in a Havana minute anytime. For without her expert coordinating skills, I would have been lost, literally. I will be forever glad she was part of our team in Cuba.

•

TEAM TACTICS FROM PROS

"First, bring together the very best 'community' you can. For me this meant inviting a core of 'uber-professionals' to help the production (they came in from over the globe!), adding students from the best film tech college here in the UK, and then leavening the whole mix - cast, crew, catering, extras, production teams - with a river of friends, acquaintances, local folks.

"In the end your film lives and dies by the quality of the team you surround yourself with.

"Second, in your mind divide this community into a core who bring strategic gifts and assets, and those who bring mainly tactical gifts.

"For example, one of our executive producers usually produces huge blockbuster films. When he asked what could he contribute to the party, I was very specific - lights, cameras and stunt men. He brought Panavision onboard - and our stunt team made available to us the days they weren't working on Ridley Scott's 'Robin Hood'.

"In other words, he made a huge professional investment in our 'little' film. That was because we have a long standing professional relationship AND he liked the script. But his strategic input was absolutely critical on every level."

- Bart Gavigan, Spark Productions

"When building a team: 'A happy crew' doesn't always mean a successful project. Keep your crew comfortable and safe, but remember that creative clash of ideas can be good - provided that everyone is out for the best product and not themselves.

"Secondly, it's imperative that there be a chain of command. This is not the same as a chain of respect. The lowliest PA works hard and performs an important function and deserves no less respect than the Executive in Charge of Production. Disrespect the Runner and you may endure the consequences when you go to review your project only to find it's gone missing."

- Bill Pruitt, supervising producer, NBC Universal

"An army travels on its stomach. Feed your crew well, and they will kill for you.

"Know what each member of the crew is responsible for and relate to them in those terms. Don't bend a gaffer's ear about a grip issue.

"Work hard yourself. Help crew members when you can. If you show them that you are willing to work hard, they will work hard.

"Meet with all the keys extensively beforehand and give them your vision of what you want to accomplish and why.

"If someone has a better idea than you, be strong enough to use it AND give them credit.

"Be prepared on the set. If a crew senses you are unprepared, they will go into a less efficient mode.

"Listen to your keys. They want to help you. Let them.

"Be nice to everyone on the set, from the DP to the lowest PA. It creates a productive, calm atmosphere.

"You can attract more flies with honey than with vinegar."

- David Carr, Beantown Productions

"On extended production trips, if it's at all possible, always allow the crew a 'laundry day' somewhere. Clean clothes make a huge difference in crew morale. And feed them well. Tired + hungry = irritated, which translates to a rapid decline in quality."

- Alan Lloyd, lighting cameraman

"When possible, hire people that are better than you are."

- Bruce Bennett, executive producer, Creative Inspiration

CHAPTER 9 REVIEW: COLLEAGUES & CREW

1. The right team of people on your project is extremely critical to its very success.
2. Filmmaking (production) by its very nature is a collaborative process.
3. Hiring people who are better than you at their crafts is a sure sign of security and confidence.
4. Using talented people should never be considered a luxury or rarity, but a basic necessity.
5. Be aware that insensitivity and cynicism can ruin almost any shoot or project.
6. When you pick a great team, with the right people doing the right jobs, everyone wins.
7. Should you be in a position to hire support staff for a project or to crew a shoot, it's best to do a little homework first. View their work, ask around.
8. Hire team members with excellent attitudes and a good work ethic - who are likable and reliable.

CHAPTER 10: CAMERA

Stand Still & Shoot

•

"Shoot a few scenes out of focus.

I want to win the best foreign film award."

- Billy Wilder, writer-director

(Some Like It Hot!, Stalag 17, The Apartment, Sabrina)

Let's be honest, there are dozens of great, professional production books that will teach you how to frame a solid shot. They artistically describe proper composition of objects/subjects in the frame, how to zoom and focus, where to place the camera, how to understand angles. Find a book you really like, read it, then try the author's suggestions. Watch films, shows or documentaries you enjoy and respect, pay attention to their shooting and editing styles, use their techniques and approach where it makes sense. But remember, you want to develop a distinct style you can truly call your own.

Still photography is a wonderful medium to educate one's artistic sensibilities for framing a good shot. I've found the better you become at still photos, the more competent you get at digital video, and vice versa. Developing a "photographer's eye" is what it's all about. As your knowledge increases, so will your abilities to place the camera in the very best spot. Of course, still photos are not film or video, for they freeze a mere moment in time. The dynamic for digital video or film is that people and objects move - at 24, 30 or 60 fps (frames per second).

But good composition is just that - good composition, plain and simple. So, the best advice I can possibly give you about shooting comes down to some crucial, but simple fundamentals.

CLOSE-UPS: Get close to your subject - maybe four to seven feet away. *Close-ups* (chest or shoulders up) are the name of the game. A person *faraway* is rarely as visually interesting as someone *close*.

FRAMING: Frame a good shot. If you can, place your subject at the side (1/2 or 1/3) of the frame - camera left or right - so the viewer can see the whole picture setting, especially if you are shooting in 16:9 (letterbox) aspect ratio. Frame a *master shot*, hold it. If you are going to attempt a move, then zoom in, hold long, zoom out (pull), hold long. Pans can be good too, holding the shot long before the pan and after you stop. Make your camera moves smooth. Feel free to *practice* the moves before committing them to tape or memory.

ACTION: There are usually two ways to bring action or energy to a shot. People and objects who are moving within the frame are best. In most cases, frame a good steady shot and let their movement occur. If people or objects are *static* (still, without movement) then a camera move (zoom, pan or walkup) will usually bring energy. Pick the framing that is appropriate for your shot.

FOCUS: Remember, especially with HD, *focus is critical*!!! Even today, I have seen segments on network shows and local news where the background is in focus but the person speaking is blurry. Focus. Take your lens OFF of auto focus and, instead, focus on the object or subject that's most important to your shot and story. Then reframe.

TRIPOD: Invest in a good tripod, buying the best you can afford. Tripods make a tremendous difference. And your "sticks" should be much heavier than you might expect. I've owned two German made Sachtlers - excellent.

STABILIZER: If your camera has an image stabilizer, use it when shooting handheld. It will reduce the shake of the shot as you move, balance or breathe. When on a tripod, turn the stabilizer OFF, as it often confuses the camera when you attempt pans or zooms. Unfortunately, leaving the stabilizer on (while on tripod) produces a *drag effect* with the stabilizer trying to overcompensate for your camera move.

MOVEMENT: Keep your moves (zooms, pans, etc.) to a minimum. Only execute a move if you have a legitimate reason, i.e., if it is part of your coverage plan of the scene. Framing a good, steady, on-the-tripod shot is almost always preferable to shaky shots and handheld - unless the scene calls for energy. Know that a steady, well-framed shot is far easier to edit too.

RECORD LONG: Hold your shots long, which means to count until at least ten seconds when shooting in *record* mode. Start *record* early, *finish* the shot late. Because you may need the extra screen time to find the best section of the footage to use; three to four second quick shots are extremely hard to edit and will frustrate you, your editor and your audience. You want *fat* shots, footage that has lots of pre-roll and post-roll before and after the section you might use in a sequence.

PRACTICE: Before tackling an important project with a new camera, go out and practice shooting something easy, like a simple stand up interview or gathering cutaway footage. First, try your camera both handheld and on a tripod. Playback your footage on a reliable monitor, so you'll know on a larger video screen - not just the viewfinder - what you're capturing. It's perfectly okay to stick to the basics when breaking in a new camera, for you are getting a "feel" for how it shoots and records images.

GEAR: Make sure every little item in your camera package is checked and prepped before you roll into production or go out on a specific shoot. Create a reliable equipment list - that includes lights, sound, batteries and cables too - then check off items before heading to the project.

WORKFLOW: Confirm that the editing workflow for your project is going to match and support the tape or memory recording format to be used. This also includes anticipated frame rate, desired aspect ratio, filters (or not) and color temperature. Before commencing production, make sure your editor and you are on the same page artistically and technically. Shooting formats and editing should work together successfully as partners.

KNOW YOUR TOOLS: Experiment with settings, menus, filters and effects so that you will know the ABC's of how to use your camera effectively. That way when you are in a time crunch or under pressure, you will work confidently. This comes down to a larger approach: know your tools. Overall, it's always better to make mistakes on shoots small and unimportant than to risk experimenting on a valuable project using an unknown camera (with lots of unfamiliar buttons).

MICROPHONES: Gauge your camera's sound capabilities too, including how loud sounds (street) and subtle sounds (nature) are recorded. Sometimes when I am shooting in the field or out on the street by myself, I will set one audio channel to a low setting, the other channel to high. That way I am fully covered either way by loud or soft sounds that occur on the fly. These contrasting settings give me audio choices when editing, even when one channel might be distorted by an unexpected noise.

•

GUERILLA SHOOTING

Over the years, I have shot in dozens of countries without a permit, and have been pretty successful. (I also have acquired the skills to talk my way out of most trouble.) When you are a small crew with just a handful of equipment and few people, your group can often fly under the radar of some officials and police. That camera gear has shrunk in size has been immensely helpful too.

But know this: **camera crews usually attract attention.**

And there is only so much creative talking you can offer to get past the gate or checkpoint before getting stopped or shutdown.

My suggestions for guerilla shooting are these:

1. **At major monuments, museums and any official buildings, it will be difficult to shoot without expressed, written permission from a government or tourism agency of some sort.** Yes, your hidden camera in the backpack might get you through, but security cameras are everywhere these days. Be prepared to be stopped. (Like when I began shooting without a permit outside London's Buckingham Palace.) So, if you are successful, count your blessings. But taking a little time to get a permit will allow you valuable access...and time.

2, Whenever possible, **hire someone local who knows your location well**, a person who can also arrange reliable transportation and secure permits. If overseas, it's vital you find someone who speaks the local language and reads the associated alphabet. Their cost per day will more than pay for itself in the experience and knowledge they will provide to your project. Don't speak Ukrainian while shooting in Kiev? Find someone who does, and, if possible, understands the nature of TV production too. The internet is filled with great crew and production web sites for at least 100+ countries. Mandy.com is one of them. Do your homework and get a local coordinator to assist you, even if your primary intent is to "wing it" without permits.

3. **Be truthful.** Never, ever lie about your intentions for the shoot or make up some story that defies logic. That doesn't mean you need to exaggerate or spill every detail to an official when asked. Only provide as much information as necessary. But be honest. It's called integrity.

4. **Have a plan before heading out to shoot.** My cameraman, Steve, and I talked about where in Moscow's *Red Square* we wanted to setup and shoot, knowing that we'd have no more than one to two minutes to photograph our zoom shots of the *Kremlin* and *St. Basil's Cathedral* before being shutdown. We recorded our two planned shots, then were shooed away by KGB security just as we finished. One of sequences ended up in the final show we were producing. Even if you're going with a seat-of-the-pants approach, think ahead as to which shots are most important, plus where to stand and when to record.

5. **Never go alone.** Take someone with you who can watch your back and protect you.

6. **Sometimes it's easier to say you're sorry, then to ask permission.**

•

KENYA, EAST AFRICA

My cameraman, Mike, and I were walking the streets of busy, bustling Nairobi on-assignment one late afternoon. Working our way past shops and bus stops, we wandered upon a small group of Kenyan men who were happily chatting away while sipping hot tea.

Realizing it was a good people/cultural shot, I asked Mike to roll some video. Standing far away, about seventy-five feet, he zoomed in and tried to hold the shot. I quickly said, "you have to get closer, Mike." He looked back at me puzzled, and said, "what, you mean go up to them?" "Yes," I responded. He was a bit afraid to do so in a foreign country, so he handed the camera to me as if to say, "show me what you mean."

Walking to about 10 feet away from the Kenyans, I smiled, said hello and asked their permission for a "photo." They smiled back and indicated, "Sure." I started with a group shot, then some singles of the men held steady and long. Followed by a slow pan, a zoom in and out. Done. Colorful, interesting, visual. It never made the final segment, but I still remember years later that dynamic between Mike (a very talented cameraman) and myself: You mean get closer? Yes.

My experience of walking through hundreds of cities and villages has taught me you usually have to get *close* to people to capture good shots. You cannot stand one hundred feet away and expect to click off good, steady shots that will be so dynamic that the video editor will argue artistically with the director that the faraway shaky shot *must* remain in the picture.

Getting close often means that you are walking into someone's *personal space*. Yes, you may think, that's both a risk, and a danger. I suggest engaging them, be nice, smile, ask their permission. You will come away with far superior footage when you get to within four to seven feet of people than playing it safe from fifty feet away.

Sure, over the years I've had a few people who got gruff, weren't extremely happy with my request for a "photo opportunity", and who made trouble. If I sensed a real problem, I would simply move on. The argument or potential for harm wasn't worth it. But I've also captured some intriguing people shots, too, that would never have been accomplished by framing from a faraway distance.

Get closer. No risk, no reward.

•

SHOOTING TIPS BY THE NUMBERS

1. **Choose the proper shooting style.** If your audience is older - 40+ in years - a fast MTV style for your shoot might only confuse and frustrate them in your storytelling. Stick to the basics with shots on the tripod. Conversely, if your intended audience is young, than quick zooms, fast pans and focus in/out shots might work. Younger viewers are used to an edgier style. *Pick the camera style and editing approach that is appropriate for your story and viewers.*

2. **Understand your genre.** How you shoot a travel show in Barbados is decidedly different than how you tackle investigative journalism delving into a charity group's financial corruption. A sports profile of David Beckham is nothing like a science documentary exploring why the frog population has begun to disappear along Minnesota's lakes. A docu-journal about living among tribal peoples in Borneo is not a short independent feature shot by friends after film school who hope to gain some buzz and awards on the festival circuit. Know your genre. Be willing to experiment with the form (Quentin Tarantino does this repeatedly by mixing genres). Engaging with the form you're producing within brings certain audience expectations. So know, and consider, these dynamics before you ever hit record.

3. **ASL - Average Shot Length.** *Keep it moving.* Unless the content from interviews and the personalities of the subjects are so engaging that long takes are possible, your segment should be paced with an ASL that works. Too many talking heads can be boring. Cutaway shots (b-roll) illustrating their comments and other visuals to enhance the narration and story keep viewers from changing the channel, or worse, becoming bored. Too quick (one second edits) can hinder you too, for the shot goes by so fast that viewer

comprehension proves difficult. *Find a beat pattern appropriate for cutting your segment that fits the words, pauses, music, pictures and sound.*

4. **Capture a Master Shot.** It should be a cardinal sin not to shoot a *Master Shot,* a basic wide shot with all the elements, action or subjects in the frame. I usually shoot this first - before any other closer setup - so that A) I have coverage of the scene for editing purposes. In addition, the master shot can also paint the scene for the viewer. Once they know the overall setting, you can cut to angles and close-ups all you want. You have framed the picture in the mind of the viewer. B) So the players can work out their staging. Or you can place your subject properly for the interview. C) So I can see how the segment will work framed wide before deciding on the proper close-ups, reactions and other possible closer angles. Work from outside/in - start wide to medium to close.

5. Know that in **High Definition** your audience can now see every little detail, even faraway in the background. So, when shooting a master shot, consider every object within the frame.

6. **Capture as much b-roll as time and budget will allow.** Better to have far too many shots and footage to choose from than not enough. *Show* me more often than you *Tell* me.

7. **Understand Shooting Ratios.** The average amount of footage needed for a standard documentary is a shooting ratio of about 25 to 1, meaning for every 1 minute of screen time, you'll need 25 minutes of raw footage. It's been written that the legendary director, Alfred Hitchcock, had the tightest shooting ratio in Hollywood - averaging 3 to 1. He was able to do this because he was so thoroughly prepared with script and storyboards. Plus, he knew what he wanted before the lights were turned on, they loaded the film magazine and the actors arrived on set. Production was boring to him, it was the pre-production that was stimulating.

For the *Unreached People* series I usually shot about 20-25 hours of footage (40-50 half hour betacam cassettes) to boil down for a 20 minute documentary. That's about a 60 to 1 ratio (1200 recorded minutes ÷ 20 screen minutes.) With my 40 cassettes (20 hours), I had a bounty of great usable footage (tons of b-roll) and plenty of solid interviews, with the editing luxury of picking my very best shots and sound bites for the final program.

On *The Amazing Race*, approximately 80-90 digital 60 minute cassettes would be shot for each location stop. Do the math: 80 cassettes for a 1 hour show is 80 to 1. Ok, perhaps not every cassette had 60 minutes recorded. Let's make it 70 to 1, which is still ample.

You need enough footage to shoot and produce your segment or story with the justice it should deserve.

That's it for camera shooting? Yes. My advice is to grab a camera, then get out there and shoot. Trial, error - mistakes and success - will teach you. (Or consider hiring talented, experienced cinematographers you can learn from.) Read the camera manual to begin, load a cassette/card, find a good story - and start shooting.

•

SHOOTING TACTICS FROM PROS

"The cameraman's camera should have behind its lens the eye of a poet."

- Orson Welles, famous filmmaker

"K.I.S.S. - Keep It Simple Stupid. Directing or Producing or shooting should be kept to an easy 'get it done' format; then if the budget and time allow, go ahead and do the creative shots and setups. Grandma in Iowa doesn't care about the shot, just the character and the acting!!

"Always try to get '2 eyes' on the person facing your camera on cross shots (over the shoulder angle)...unless the logistics on camera placement are confining. Seeing only '1 eye' of a profile is not as visually interesting."

- Michael J. Denton, network cameraman

"*Camera focus* - it's one of the few things you can't fix in post-production."

- Joe Sindorf, freelance producer-director

"Always get more b-roll (cover) footage than you think (you'll need it).

"For more dramatic type pieces use tripods when possible. Many times handheld shots can drain the emotion out of a piece.

"Take advantage of your camera if it shoots at 60 fps (frames per second). Your slow-mo shots will look very smooth compared to slowing it down in post. You can always speed it up with no ill effects if you need it at regular speed."

- Steve Taylor, Digital Spatula

"Use a tripod wherever and whenever you can, and hire a gaffer - that way you will get a professional look."

- Martina Nagel, writer & cinematographer

"Learn the KISS (Keep It Simple Stupid) principle.

"Treat every take with the respect it deserves.

"Someone said 'every take should have a beginning, a middle and an end - even if it's only a few seconds long' - all the rest belong in the bin.

"On a live shoot you can never have enough batteries.

"Tape was cheap - memory is cheaper.

"Gaffer (duct) tape is cheap.

"You can never have enough Sharpies.

"You are in *record* - right??

"A blanket or a bath mat may quiet a noisy camera.

"It doesn't matter how cold *you* are - it does matter how cold the *equipment* is."

- Derek Murray, Cfan

"Don't tie up your capital buying a camera and related kit. Hire it by the day or week as you may need. Today's digital video hardware is obsolete before a startup company can fully amortize it."

- Eric Braun, Associated Press

"Start making movies, plain and simple. Hopefully, over time, the filmmaker will start to understand how to tell a story which is the essence of filmmaking. It's not about technology and all the latest gear. It's about telling a story, evoking emotions from the viewer and it's much harder than it sounds even with the best gear.

"I went to USC film school for 3 years and spent $75,000 in the 1990's, and I wish someone had told me that before I spent a lot of money on gear that was obsolete 5 years later. "

- Mark Berger, Stock-Track Group

"If you're going to buy any sort of gear, go buy yourself a good tripod. Cameras and formats go in and out of style, but a good tripod is always needed.

"It should weigh enough that you don't like carrying it. (Carry it anyway!) It should have both locks and drags for both pan and tilt, as well as an adjustable counterbalance setting and the ability to slide the wedge plate back and forth to fine-tune the balance of your rig du jour. You should also have to use both hands to defeat an interlock, and slide - not lift - the wedge plate out of the tripod head. It's safer that way, trust me. And a leveling ball and bubble are essential - leveling a tripod by messing with the legs is no fun.

"And if the tilt lock control is on the tilt axis of rotation, DO NOT BUY IT! (Yes, I'm looking at you, Manfrotto tripods!)

"Handheld is good, and I love shooting off the shoulder, but for important stuff, you want to be on tripod legs. Solid, dependable, trustworthy legs."

- Alan Lloyd, lighting cameraman

"Whenever possible, steady the camera by using a tripod, or by leaning against a wall, a car, or a railing.

"Limit your camera movement: Footage that never stops moving is useless for editing..

"Manual focus: If your camera has manual focus, consider using it often. Automatic focus often keeps shifting, especially if there are moving objects in the foreground, or in dim light.

"Make sure to take a couple of establishing or wide shots of the activity, then move in closer for some medium shots and, finally, shoot close-up shots of people and action. And stay on each shot for at least a 10-count!

"Get plenty of close-ups. Video thrives on expressive faces that reveal character and moods. Close-ups heighten the emotional appeal of your video - be generous with them!"

- Stan Jeter, CBN News

"If you're a really small crew - say a team of one - then you need to create a method for how you'll stash your unused equipment and carrying bags while you're shooting so that you will be able to 1) pack up quickly and 2) leave a room knowing that you have everything you came with.

"My own personal practice was to pick a point fairly deep into the room as my point of origin. Ideally, it would be out of the way of any shot I wanted to compose. From that point, I'd back out of the room following a shoot and the packing of my equipment. While doing so, I'd tick off all the nooks and crannies I had used during the shoot making sure that nothing belonging to me was still in the room.

"This might seem like a needlessly complicated thing to do. But when your crew is small (or it's just you) you don't want to leave behind a piece of equipment (no matter how seemingly inconsequential). Sure, you can buy a new set of double-A batteries or replace your tape stock. But do you really want to create that hurdle for yourself when there are more important production matters to deal with?"

- Tim Adkins, media content developer

"Know your workflow in advance! Think through every, single, small detail. Map out a day of shooting in your head - mentally go through every scenario you could come across.

"Be creative and flexible when it comes to lighting and sound: sometimes that lamp in the corner can be repositioned as a spot or fill.

"Can you use a shotgun for situations where a wireless is impractical?

"Can you rent it local vs. carrying it with you?

"Can you get by with less? Do you really 'need' that 35mm adapter kit? Or other lenses?"

- Jay Freisen, media producer, Peacemaker Ministries

"Make sure you got the shot. If you didn't get it, you don't have it. If in doubt, check. Better yet shoot it again if you can.

"Also, seems like a no-brainer, but in the heat of things it can be easy to overlook: use headphones when the audio you're capturing is important (i.e. interviews or environmental noise.) Just because it sounds good to your ears doesn't mean that your camera is picking it the same way you do.

"My last bit of advice is this: microphone cables are an annoyance in a shot. Take time to hide them. Have your subject slip them under their shirt or beneath their jacket if possible. Be creative. Taking the time to deal with that can be the difference between saving a shot and ruining one."

- Chris Northcross, media fellow, House Democratic Caucus

"If you are shooting the film yourself, or if you are the videographer, make sure you check the basics on every shot. When you are stressed, rushed, tired, you can miss the simple little things.

"I have been shooting on video for 15+ years, and I still have a little checklist in my camera case.

"White balance. Exposure. Focus.

"Audio, can you hear it, enough level, background noise?

"Is there a tape in the camera?

"Test record on every tape.

"Did you push record?

"Is the tape running?

"Slate each shot/take.

"A little notebook and clapping hands work as well as a slate board."

- Bill Moede, video/media producer

"I was an aerial combat videographer and a producer/director for 12 years in the Air Force. A majority of my projects were actually deployments (to include war zones) and while you plan as much as possible, a majority of the action is uncontrolled, much like documentary filmmaking.

"The best advice I could give to someone getting started is to be as fundamentally sound as possible. Learn the basics so well that they're second nature. By basics, I mean knowing ALL your camera functions on manual, shot sequences, cutaways, editing in camera as much as possible, exposures/filters, and, of course, audio. When these tasks become automatic, then you can give a majority of your attention to the subject and anticipating the action.

"Also, learn how to stabilize your camera and shots by any means necessary. A tripod is essential, but also be aware of your surroundings and the different ways you can get creative and professional looking shots. The floor, a table, bags, lean against a wall or a tree, even cradle the camera like a baby. A favorite of mine when I'm shooting action is to use a monopod. So many times I see a camera op just push record and follow the action.

"Finally, remember, while the story is the most important thing...presenting it in the most professional and unobtrusive way will get your audience to invest in that story even more!"

- Juan Fernath, producer-director

CHAPTER 10 REVIEW: CAMERA

1. Get closer. No risk, no reward.
2. Know your tools.
3. Use a tripod.
4. Make sure shooting format matches editing workflow.
5. Pick the camera style and editing approach that is appropriate for your story and viewers.
6. Understand your genre.
7. Keep the pace moving on average shot length.
8. Get a Master Shot.
9. Capture as much b-roll as time and budget will allow.
10. Understand Shooting Ratios.
11. Your audio is as important as your video.
12. Focus is critical.
13. Hold your shots long.

CHAPTER 11: LIGHTING

Let There Be Light!

•

"Where is the light?"

- Ed Nelson, October 1985

Decades later, I can still remember Ed's powerful words regarding light, can sense the simple setting, a casual business dinner at a Sacramento, CA airport hotel. Can recall, just mere moments after Ed (my key client) spoke those crucial words, that I didn't have much of a clue what he was truly talking about.

Shame on me, for I had been working in the television production world for about 8 years by then, mostly as a creative person producing, directing and writing. I should have - certainly by that time - understood the critical importance of light, especially its position. But I didn't, even though I had guessed and fumbled my way through lighting plenty of interviews, meetings and setups.

Understanding the strategic importance - and essential meaning - of Ed's words forever changed both my artistic abilities in directing, and my creative approach to camera work. Properly considering light - including its color temperature, intensity, placement and direction - launched me on a journey to become much more proficient at my art and craft. The production quality and the aesthetics of both my shooting on-camera and lighting a scene increased dramatically. Ed's short, but very powerful phrase sparked it all.

Six months before meeting with Ed, he had given me a plum assignment traveling to exotic Bangkok, Thailand with a cameraman friend, Steve Boggess, a graduate of UCLA's well-respected film school. Early one morning in Bangkok, Steve and I were shooting outside a Buddhist temple recording b-roll footage of Thai monks. Wearing shaved heads, dressed in orange saffron robes, these holy men (most of them young) emerged through their ancient monastery's large wooden door, then quietly swept through a courtyard to walk the nearby streets. Stopping along the way, their devoted Thai followers would offer these monks bowls of food and rice as meal gifts.

While we were shooting footage, I asked Steve to grab some shots of the monks walking across the dark courtyard. Steve turned around to me and mentioned that the group was heavily "back lit", a descriptive term which I barely understood. What Steve was attempting to explain to me was that in the early morning light the monks would hardly be recognizable in the footage. Puzzled, I said a quick okay, so we moved on.

Months later, back in the USA, it suddenly dawned on me - upon hearing Ed's words - *exactly* what Steve was talking about that day: The morning sun was in the *wrong place* for the courtyard sequence to work photographically, because it was low on the horizon *behind* the monks, not in *front* of them. Back lit shots of the holy men walking outside of the temple were hardly going to work, even if I, as director, insisted on it.

"Where is the light?" is one of the most important principles I can offer you for your lighting and shooting virtually any sequence. For light is either your friend...or an enemy (like time).

I could write an entire instructional narrative in this chapter about the color temperature of sundown, sun up and midday, could explain how most city street lights are sodium, thus giving off a yellowish, unflattering glare. That tungsten light is whiter and cleaner, and fluorescent used indoors in many offices, buildings and shops can appear green or gray (and unappealing) on-camera.

Years later I have the hard-earned experience to describe where to place a key light, a back light, a fill and a kick. I know how to use a dimmer pack, and have learned the strategic importance of plugging separate lights into spaced plugs using extension cords that run to individual circuits (so not to trip the breakers). Am able to explain to you that "golden time" can transform even *The Elephant Man* from grotesque to great on-camera. But I won't. It's best to leave it to the experts. Know that others, who are far more experienced, astute, artistic and gifted, have written great books on the subject and taught sessions on proper lighting techniques. However, I believe you will - by trial, error, mistakes and success - figure it out too.

Strategically, what I will tell you are some of the fundamentals:

LOCATION: *Know where the light is.* It is usually divided between *natural* (sun, moon, stars) or *artificial* (man made). Each of these primary sources can uniquely help or hinder you. When they are mixed, one must adjust with orange or blue gels...or change the bulbs from outdoor to indoor.

SOURCES: Learn specifically how to employ *every possible light source* to your production's distinct advantage.

NATURAL: If natural, then overcast, bounce, fill and shade will assist you, as will reflectors, silks and white cards. *When on-location, know when and where the sun is rising, arcing and setting.* Understand that overcast clouds can be your best friends, unless they portend rain, lightning or thunder.

ARTIFICIAL: For artificial, *learn how to use a lighting kit, gaffer truck or portable camera light.* Don't know what works or how? Experiment or, better yet, hire a professional DP or Gaffer. Learn from them by observing and asking questions. Let them teach and guide you. Along the way, you will find that gels, soft boxes, reflectors, snoots and diffusion will become your friends. You'll eventually need to know how industrial light works too, from warehouses to stores to offices.

LEARN: *Invest in either a lighting class or, at least, a textbook on film and television lighting.* Consider attending local seminars or workshops. Also consider buying a good, basic lighting kit, if budget allows. I purchased a Lowell DP kit years ago that has proven to be a solid investment. Later, I added dimmer packs, chimeras and other assorted cosmetics to transform my basic, original kit into a valuable package I now use to *paint* a scene professionally and artistically. The kit and extras added have turned into money very well-spent.

ADDITIONAL LIGHT: Many of my overseas shoots have taken me to difficult places featuring extremely low light inside dark huts, one bulb churches and orphanages, or dim back alleys. My purchase of a simple, but effective $75 Canon sun gun (on-board camera light) has paid dividends many times over. This small, portable 20 watt light operates on rechargeable batteries (that match my camera) and weighs virtually nothing.

I have found that the beam does throw a very strong spotlight up close, so I often put some diffusion across the light to soften its intensity, and I dial my camera settings to *spotlight* mode to compensate. But, if I am using a small crew or traveling as a one man band, the mounted camera light has saved me multitudes of time and heartache in dark conditions. And, when pressed, it can be used extensively at night too for one person stand ups *news style*.

•

BENIN, WEST AFRICA

In 2002, I tackled a very challenging shoot on voodoo ceremonies in Africa. My dear friend, Christophe Dewanou, was familiar with where voodoo practices were often held outside Benin's capital of Cotonou. One night we went exploring in four wheel drive vehicles, looking and listening for distant villages where drumming and dancing were happening.

Eventually, we wandered across a small, powerful tribal ceremony already taking place, but it was being conducted in a clearing with near total darkness. There was little or no electricity in the village. About a hundred people were dancing in the dark. After seeking the gracious permission from the local tribal chief to videotape his people and their rituals, we walked over to the dance circle where people were singing and chanting in a voodoo ceremony.

In a previous chapter on decision-making, I wrote about the importance of adaptability. If ever there was a need for improvisation, this was it. Nothing was planned or staged. This was winging it with a capital "W". But before recording the rituals, what was needed at that critical moment was somehow, somewhere to find some light, at least enough to shoot the sequence.

Surveying the possibilities, the only light sources I figured we could muster with no available electricity, in the middle of nowhere, in virtually pitch black conditions were...our truck lights. So we positioned our 4 wheel drive vehicles to shine their lamps at the outdoor dance group, then asked the drivers to turn everything to *high beam.*

This became my "lighting kit." I made sure the truck lights were behind or to the side of me as I worked my camera around the gyrating voodoo dancers. The entire music sequence in the award-winning documentary, *Benin: Cradle of Voodoo*, was shot entirely with truck lights, which gave off long, eerie shadows. To accomplish the individual insert shots of the nearby voodoo houses, paintings, white flag and fetish objects, I used my on-board camera light. In a pinch, it all worked brilliantly.

Adapt, improvise.

•

LIGHTING TIPS BY THE NUMBERS

1. Learn and master the art of **3 Point Lighting**. Key light, back light, fill light.

- The *key* light is behind or just to the side of the primary camera.
- *Back* light is opposite of the key (behind and to the opposite side of the subject). The back light is focused on a person's shoulders and back of head. It is sometimes a lesser strength bulb that helps define the space between the background and the person being photographed.
- The *fill* light is to the side, filling in the gap between key and back light. The fill's placement is meant to compliment the person and smooth out shadows.

Don't know how to achieve 3 Point Lighting? Have a gaffer or lighting cameraman show you. You can shoot with two lights, but this setup will rarely let you down when lighting an interview.

2. **Recognize which is a person's "good" side, then have their screen direction and lighting feature that side.** Many times, someone's best side is where someone parts their hair (though

not always). My good side is my left, so I would feature that on-screen by looking camera direction left (stage right). The majority of the time, light the subject with the key light directed toward their best side. This common setup is called "broad" lighting.

3, **Hiring an experienced lighting director or gaffer will enhance your project tremendously.** Learn from them, watch where they place lights and ask why. If possible, communicate before the shoot as to what you want to accomplish, the physical location, subjects featured and the look you desire. If the "LD" is any good - and most are - let them make creative, practical suggestions to help shape your vision.

4, **Use a reputable, professional lighting store.** Find a knowledgeable sales assistant - someone with lighting experience - and let them guide and advise you. Be very clear as to the type of production requirements you anticipate, and whether yours is a simple, straightforward shoot, complicated setup or a studio production. Create a wish list of lights, accessories and cosmetics (gels, diffusion etc.) you'd like eventually to purchase that will enhance future shoots.

5, **If you can't afford to purchase, then rent.** Again, consider hiring a professional gaffer that will bring his/her own lighting package to your shoot for a rental fee. Gaffers - or lighting camerapersons - often have built a trusty "bag of tricks" that's filled with little goodies that expand your production's possibilities.

6. **Chimera lights** (soft boxes) will flatter your subject and give your shoot a very up-to-date, professional look. Next best are umbrellas, which can be setup and folded away quickly.

7. **Cookies** (cut out patterns) will give a great patterned beam on the back wall that compliments the subjects being interviewed. Most any professional network sit-down interview will employ cookies for their background, for they provide a high-end *portrait* look.

8. **C-stands** are the workhorses of lighting. If you shoot regularly enough to afford and justify the cost, purchase a good set of three to four C-stands. Sometimes, you can find them *used* for a fraction of the price *new*. Buy arms and grip heads, so that you can

place back lights above and away from the heads of your subjects. Purchase *sand bags*, too, that will safely hold the stands weight down. Nothing is worse than an unbalanced C-stand with a hot light on it that topples over crashing onto someone or something important.

9. **Kino Flo Diva** lights are a great, professional toy that can be setup quickly and efficiently. The bulbs can be switched out for indoor or outdoor shoots, thus saving having to blue gel a scene. Diva lights also have dimmer switches attached, so it's a simple way to dial in the proper intensity.

10. **Wooden clothes pins** (or clamps) are a great way to clip diffusion (tough spun) and gels. Never buy plastic pins as they melt with the light's heat.

11. **Bring spare bulbs.** More than you need. Always use a kleenex to change out the bulbs, as the oils from your fingers will create a hot spot that burns quickly on the bulb, reducing its life. *And remember to handle hot lights with work gloves.*

12. **Diffusion is your friend.** *Tough Spun* is the best known and most used. Clipped to a light's barn doors, diffusion will make most any harsh light softer in intensity. Double it over to make it even softer.

13. **Dimmer packs are ideal to adjust the strength of the lights...and necessary.** I went to a *Home Depot* store and bought all the basic parts for four dimmer packs. Then I had an electrician friend build them for me at a fraction of the cost for expensive name brand dimmers.

14. **You can never have enough long, thick extension cords** (called stingers).

15. **Gaffer tape.** I like black. Some use gray. Doesn't matter. Buy a couple of big rolls. Know that a roll often lasts a long time.

16. **Indoor light is red/orange. Outdoor light is blue.** *Blue gels* (1/4 or 1/2 strength) are necessary when matching indoor shots with available outdoor light. *Orange gels* are necessary to correct outdoor setups when the primary light is coming from *indoors*.

17. **Black wrap,** similar to aluminum foil but much stronger, can be placed around barn doors to cover light spills. Black wrap can also be formed into tube like snoots that will focus your light where you want and need it.

18. A good, easy to pack **pop reflector** (silver on one side, white on the other) that can be folded up is both a lifesaver and money very well-spent. I have owned the same $65 Photoflex brand reflector for more than two decades and it's been to at least fifty countries. Outdoors, a reflector is ideal for filling in shadows, using sunlight as an advantage. One can also use it - or a large white card - for filling in areas "under lit" when indoors by placing it opposite or to the side of your key light. One can also clamp a reflector to a c-stand and swivel it to adjust for proper placement.

19. Remember, it's **what the camera sees** - not your own eyes - that is most important in lighting and color temperature.

There are potential pages with many more possible tricks and tactics that can transform your shoot to look better and more professional. But this basic rundown, plus other creative, practical tactics, will serve you well for now.

Lighting is both challenging and fun, with creative possibilities that seem endless. And remember to use a good *video monitor* that will represent accurately what your physical shoot is showing with the lighting setup. Don't be lazy by relying only on your camera's viewfinder.

Feel free, artistically and photographically, to experiment with different setups of light placement, intensity and cosmetics to light a scene. But know that learning and mastering the 3 light setup will rarely, if ever, steer your production wrong.

•

LIGHTING TACTICS FROM PROS

"Someone much smarter than me once said, 'the light you have available is the best light in the world.' Learn how to use it to your advantage."

- Derek Murray, Cfan

“To understand light: Go to art museums and spend time looking at Flemish masters' paintings. Serious time. Look at what they did with light and shadows. Look again. Reflect, and look some more. Try to recreate the look. It may not be what you're shooting next week, but it will make you better at lighting.

“If you have an extended outdoor shooting schedule, have a decent idea of where the sun is going to be when, and time things accordingly if you can. Nothing is worse than someone silhouetted against a blown out background, and there isn't always budget for HMI's and a generator. A 4-by double net will help some if there's room for it, and there are collapsible frames for such things if the vehicle is small. Just make sure it's far enough behind your talent and that you're far enough back to throw the net soft, or more will result.”

- Alan Lloyd, lighting cameraman

“Many times a reflector or white card are all you need (especially when you have no power). Indoors, bounce your light off a white wall or ceiling for a softer effect.”

- Steve Taylor, Digital Spatula

“News-worthy events are not always well-lit, but please do make the effort to shoot under good lighting when you can. It is best not to shoot into a light source like a window behind your subject, but instead move so that the light source is behind you. Many home video cameras can produce almost professional looking video in well-lit situations.”

- Stan Jeter, CBN News

“If you need to do an interview outside, but you're dealing with harsh sunlight, and you must shoot *now* - take a white bed sheet and hoist it up somehow to soften the light falling on your subject.”

- Aaron Burns, producer-editor

CHAPTER 11 REVIEW: LIGHTING

1. "Where is the light?"
2. Adapt, improvise.
3. Learn and master the art of *3 Point Lighting*.
4. Recognize which is a person's "good" side.
5. Hiring an experienced lighting director or gaffer will enhance your project tremendously.
6. Use a reputable, professional lighting store.
7. *Diffusion* is your friend.
8. *Indoor* light is red/orange. *Outdoor* light is blue.
9. Bring *gels* that will color correct indoor or outdoor light.
10. Use a good *video monitor* that will represent *accurately* what your physical shoot is showing with the lighting setup.
11. Remember, it's what the *camera* sees - not your own eyes - that is most important in lighting and color temperature.

CHAPTER 12: AUDIO

Sound Principles

•

"Adding sound to movies would be like
putting lipstick on the Venus de Milo."
- Mary Pickford, producer-actress

Fortunately, Miss Pickford was wrong: lipstick works pretty well on the Venus de Milo. When Al Jolson sang to his screen mother in 1927's *The Jazz Singer*, sound was here to stay. The advent of "talkies" forever transformed the movie-going experience from silent pictures to an over-reliance on the spoken word. Dialog, sound efx and synchronous sound took over.

Yet, for most modern filmmakers today, sound is still the one vital element that gets terribly shortchanged time and again. It's because most creative people think *visual* over *sonic*. Too bad.

For decades, I have been hammering home a point that a project's sound should be every bit as professional as the pictures. Sound requires extra attention, but, when recorded and mixed properly, adds layers of production dynamics to most any segment or story. Pay close attention to sound, designing an audio approach as skillfully as you do with your visual storytelling. Your audience may not pickup on it at first, but they *do* recognize unintelligible words, garbled mistakes and uneven levels when they hear them.

Besides production in the studio or the field, post-production sound with a proper audio mix will add quality and value to your segment or film. If at all possible - unless budget and deadlines dictate otherwise - provide a proper sound mix to your project.

I'll take that back. Forget budget and deadlines. You MUST separate, layer and mix your sound when editing. Simply identify individual tracks for the music, natural sound, dialog and narration, then mix them down to stereo tracks. Such a proper audio mix will prove you're the true filmmaking professional you've always claimed you were.

Paying close attention to sound pays dividends.

Early in my career, I worked on a massive documentary project, *Unreached People.* It was a 13 episode exploration of faith and beliefs that took my small production company almost four years to produce and edit. Our crew was off to a far corner of the world every couple months, eventually shooting in forty-four countries. From the start, I was always careful and attentive to sound, using good microphones and proper placement, both for b-roll footage and standup interviews.

When production on a specific episode was completed, I would finish up the on-line edit, then go to the sound mixing suite to see my friend and colleague, Jeff Callaway (nominated for 5 *Emmys*). The extra day spent in the sound suites equalizing the voices and ambient sounds (traffic, wilderness, natural ambiance), adding the sound track, then blending it all into a good stereo mix was extra time, patience and budget money well-spent. The series *sounded* just as good and professional as it *looked* on-screen. That's what your project should accomplish too, if possible.

Record your sound properly from the start - in the field or studio - then in the final mix.

For the most part, unless you're covering a convention or event where mics are run through a sound board, there are four primary ways (though there are more) to record location or studio sound on most film, television and video productions:

- lavalieres (wireless or hard-wired)
- shotgun unidirectional mic (often with zep and fish pole)
- omnidirectional mic (handheld wireless, wired or set on a mic stand/arm)
- on-board camera microphone

One can't say enough about the importance of rarely depending on the manufacturer's on-board camera mic for field recording.

Consider swapping it out with the best shotgun mic you can afford. (Then bring the manufacturer's mic with you on shoots as a backup.) A professional shotgun mic will instantly transform your ambient sound recording from average to superior. (In my experience, you can never go wrong with Sennheiser.)

Don't know which mic to buy? Take your camera to a reputable video dealer and try out different mic setups. Ask dependable sound professionals what they would recommend for your camera. Or go online and browse what leading video and audio suppliers offer. (I like *B&H Photo Video* in New York. *Location Sound* in Burbank, CA too.) Call, ask questions and get their input before ordering.

You will also need various windscreens for your mics to cut out wind noise. Know that you can usually leave the windscreens off when recording indoors, unless you pickup scratching sounds from clothing or air conditioner noise.

Buy good quality mic cables at various lengths (10', 20') with tie wraps.

Finally, buy the best studio headphones you can afford for production. Hearing is believing.

The sound designers at the end of this chapter are far more qualified than I am to offer their opinions on recording good sound in the field, on-set and in-studio. I will add a few basic tips I've learned along the way. But, again, paying close attention to sound levels, wind noise and mic distortion while on a shoot - and correcting or adjusting it immediately - will help you tremendously when editing, resulting in a quantum leap sonically at your important final showing or for an upcoming sneak preview.

Remember: Garbage in, garbage out. Same adage applies to sound.

•

VARANASI, INDIA

It was dawn one crisp February morning as our two man camera crew stood along the dirty, crowded banks of the Ganges River in the ancient Indian city of Varanasi. We had wandered by chance into a festival day, and the ghats (steps) of this ancient, holy city were packed with devotees, literally tens of thousands of them. What Mecca is to Muslims, Varanasi is to Hindus. They are required once in their lifetime, if possible, to make a spiritual pilgrimage to these murky waters to bath and pray, for the Ganges is sacred to them. The sights and sounds are visually and sonically incredible. India is what one former colleague calls a "target rich environment," meaning that almost anywhere you point your camera, you will find a great, colorful shot.

The early morning of our production, we hired one of the simple row boats along the ghats to take us out into the river, so that we could shoot back at the horizon of temples and believers. There were just three of us in the boat: the oarsman, Steve (camera) and myself. As the oarsman pulled on the oars, I realized that the creaking sound of his rowing would be great sonically for the sequence we were shooting. Because we were gliding on water - always a great sound amplifier by its reflective nature - the sound was clear and intriguing.

With Steve shooting away while sitting and facing the oarsman, and our shotgun microphone recording the synchronous sounds, I decided to do something vitally important as the "third party" in the boat: *shut up*. I remained quiet, not making a single sound. As we recorded the rowing, we were picking up every creak of the oars as the boat pulled out into the river.

If I, as director, had spoken, the oarsman's rowing sound would have been forever ruined by my voice. Instead, we captured every slap of water made by his paddles, every boat groan as we slowly floated through the brown waters toward the horizon. Many years later, I can still hear the distinct sounds of those creaky oars.

Later that morning in Varanasi, we also recorded rice being thrown into beggars' bowls, the prayerful cries as worshippers plunged into the water, and the cacophony of crowd noises. When we returned to America to edit and prepare the sound mix, the synchronous oar sounds, rice, splashing and wails worked together in perfect harmony. All of these distinct, exotic sounds made for a great, synchronous audio mix that worked effectively in the show. *Unreached People: India* was like no other project I have shot, edited or mixed ever again.

The moral of this faraway river adventure is that there are so many times when it's best just to remain quiet, to let the camera and mics do their quality work.

Silence (by the crew) is golden when a potentially great sonic moment occurs.

By the way, the Ganges segment was used for many years as a good example in proper field sound by the *Sony Video Institute* in Hollywood. There's a feather in the cap.

•

SOUND TIPS BY THE NUMBERS

1. Clip the lavaliere on the side of the subject where they will be turning most to speak to the interviewer. Nothing is more frustrating to the sound mix than an improperly placed mic.

2. You can dress the lavaliere wire by turning it in a loop and letting the clip hold the excess from behind. Never let a wire dangle undressed down a person's shirt, blouse or tie.

3. A small piece of gaffer tape will help hide the excess wiring inside a shirt or coat.

4. If a blouse or shirt is too fragile or flimsy to hold the mic clip, try using a credit or business card clipped inside and around the back. Remember to get your credit card back after the shoot.

5. The rule is that the closer the microphone is to the speaker's mouth, usually the better the sound quality will be - doesn't matter if it's a lav or shotgun mic. (But not TOO close.)

6. If a person is wearing a tie, it's perfectly okay to clip the lav to the mid point of the tie. That way you're covered no matter which direction they turn to speak. Dress the wiring.

7. For sit-down interviews, a shot gun mic set on an arm and c-stand, held by a mini grip head, that is positioned above the subject's head (out of camera frame), will save your sound man's arm and will more than adequately do the job. Watch out for the wide shot and the over scan of Hi Def viewfinders - unless you don't mind seeing equipment.

8. If hiring a freelance crew, try to book a camera person and sound person who have worked together as a team before on previous shoots and projects. They will speak and work in a short hand that should enhance your project with simpatico, cohesion and teamwork.

9. If mounting a two camera shoot, book a sound person. Just because you have it covered with two cameras doesn't mean your audio levels will match or be wired properly.

10. Pay close attention and check your audio inputs on your camera, both exterior switches and menu settings. All it takes is one setting to be dialed in wrong to mess up sound.

11. Listen to your sound people. If they say they're picking up the airport control tower on the wireless lavs or that the mic is being scratched by someone's shirt fabric, believe them.

12. If you are directing, arrange to have your own headphones. That way you can confirm spoken voices and ambient sound...and you will hear problems as they occur just like the sound person is hearing too.

•

SOUND TACTICS FROM PROS

"If the sound quality is poor, it is almost always the best indicator that the overall production is second rate."

- Chris Bueno, Carmel Entertainment

“I use a wired lav mic when I can so that radio interference and loss of battery power are not an issue.”

- Steve Taylor, Digital Spatula

“So many newbies will run out and shoot an interview with an on-camera mic because they can't afford a wireless. The real answer for those on a budget is one of those clip-on mics from Radio Shack. Around $20. For another $5 you can get a 10 foot audio extension cord. In a pinch, you can cover a scene with two cameras and two of these mics. They sound much better than the on-camera mic. We've even aired sound captured this way on a few of our shows when we needed pickups and were out of cash, including *Beauty and the Geek* and *Scream Queens*.”

- Biagio Messina, Joke Productions

"Tip for sound: Turn off the AC, refrigerator and unplug all phones.”

- Martina Nagel, writer-cinematographer

“When you unplug the fridge to eliminate sound, put the car keys in the freezer. That way you won't forget to plug in the fridge again before you leave.”

- Martha Cotton, Plymouth Rock Studios

“Most on-camera microphones do a very good job of picking up general sounds during taping. When interviewing participants, stand very close - or if possible use a separate, handheld or lapel mic so what the person says is very clear. If you are using a separate mic, make sure you have the correct microphone adapter cord and use headphones to monitor the audio. Try playing back the segment right afterward to confirm both audio and image are good.”

- Stan Jeter, CBN News

“I've been fighting for more years than I care to count for more importance to be placed on audio.”

- Charley Buchanan, PBS cameraman

"Use natural sound and remember to record ambiance. Again, not every second of your documentary needs to be someone talking, let the film breathe and allow time for viewers to enjoy the pretty footage that you have shot.

"Music is good for setting mood and atmosphere, though don't over-use as you'll create a music video."

- Gregory Branch, producer-journalist

"Sound IS important.

"You can't always fix it in the mix.

"It's easier to turn the level up than turn the distortion down.

"As much as a director doesn't want your mic in the shot, he also doesn't want it pointing down at the road.

"Record everything - even the silence.

"Hide a distracting sound with other distracting sounds.

"Go and listen with your ears before listening with headphones.

"Don't trust the cameraman to record the sound, even if you are the cameraman.

"Always have more than one mic available.

"You can never have enough cables.

"Remember that connector you needed?

"You can never have enough ambient sounds in your library."

- Derek Murray, Cfan

"I also want to amplify the importance about natural sound. Sometimes the best storytelling is letting something happen while you're there to capture it. Shoot for a cut (wide first, then move in), and change angles and heights regularly.

"Also, let the action move both into and out of frame - this creates natural transitions for the edit. Watch your screen directions!"

- Alan Lloyd, lighting cameraman

CHAPTER 12 REVIEW: SOUND

1. Paying close attention to sound pays dividends.
2. Record your sound properly at the start - in the field or studio - then in the final mix.
3. One can't say enough about the importance of rarely depending on the manufacturer's on-board camera mic for field recording.
4. Buy the best studio headphones you can afford for production. Hearing is believing.
5. Remember: Garbage in, garbage out. Same adage applies to sound.
6. Silence (by the crew) is golden when a potentially great sonic moment occurs.
7. Listen to your sound person.

CHAPTER 13: EDITING

Killing Your Darlings

•

> "Film editing is now something almost everyone can do at a simple level and enjoy it, but to take it to a higher level requires the same dedication and persistence that any art form does."
>
> - *Walter Murch*
> *legendary film editor-sound designer*
> *(Apocalypse Now, The Godfather, The English Patient)*

The addition of this chapter on editing is somewhat new. In my original e-Book editions, I purposely omitted editing as a theme. My position then was that I was not (am not) a professional editor, but a producer, director and writer. What, I thought, could I possibly say about editing?

After hearing from scores of film students and media workshop participants over the past few years, the topic of editing has, I believe, never been as important or as popular as it is now. Much of this is due to the dramatic decrease in the cost of small, powerful computers and editing software like *Final Cut Pro*. Great compact HD cameras have never been more portable - or cheaper. In addition, buy most any *Macintosh* computer and *iMovie* comes loaded on the hard drive.

Shoot, cut, upload. You're in the video/tv game in no time. Short films, segs, clips, docs, music, sports, news, pranks - they're all available on *YouTube*, *Vimeo* and the like.

Editing must now be addressed, I feel.

In my professional infancy, when I was just barely twenty-one years old, I was pulling clips from massive 2" video reels, writing scripts, recording voice-overs and editing broadcast promos for what is now *INSP Network*. The various demands of having to tell a story - to get your point across - in just 30-60 seconds was invaluable experience in my development as a storyteller. Still is. In fact, short form videos and films are much harder to write, create and edit due to their brief running time. Every second is precious, every minute counts.

From 1977 till the 1990s, I was heavily involved in *linear* editing, all of it tape-based. Window burns, edit decision lists, sub-masters, b-roll tapes, rough cuts, on-line editing, audio sweetening, graphics and digital video efx, then it was layback, mastering and duplication. We booked expensive, by-the-hour professional edit suites run by very accomplished (or not) editors. That's how it was done then. Some excellent shows, specials, commercials, documentaries, promos and spots were produced that way, all on tape.

Then, in 1994, I jumped straight into the emerging *non-linear* (computer-based) format via *Avid* while directing *Traveling Lite: Paris* for *PBS*. All of the show's editing was done in Chicago over a two week period. Having fifteen years of *linear* experience, I quickly grasped the ease and difference represented by *non-linear*. The emerging system's random access ability - once footage was digitized - allowed for far greater creativity and possibilities. I loved it, still do.

Jumping forward to today, we are, thankfully, past even using tape for the most part. It's SD cards/storage drives and transferring footage straight into the edit system. The ability to shoot and edit quickly, creatively, holds immense promise and potential; The quality's gone up.

However, despite the numerous technological and editorial changes - now with various versions of a project - some things still remain the same.

For example, I believe that **two sets of eyes** in the edit suite are better than just one set. A good editor should come to your project with a fresh, unbiased perspective. They often are far more objective when working on your project because they haven't lived with the production process like you have. Good editors - great ones - are worth their asking price. For they have the abilities to transform that raw footage of yours into a story that moves the viewer. Or not.

I have worked with scores of truly great editors, having spent years in editing suites. The vast majority of the time, our sessions and time together have been harmonious, resulting in tremendous visual and aural storytelling on film or video.

Two sets of eyes (and ears) are better than one.

So, here are my *Top 10* basic editing tips & tactics. To be sure, it's not an end all. Others can offer twenty-seven more gems of technological and creative strategy. But, for me, this is a solid place to start. Follow this sage advice...and you'll be headed on a straight track to success in post-production.

•

TIP #1 - EDIT WHILE YOU SHOOT

Constantly be thinking of how you will edit what you're directing and shooting. In other words, try to edit while you shoot. Think in entire sequences. How will this shot work with another? Do I need a close-up, cutaway or transition? How much footage is needed to complete this project based on *Average Shot Length* (the length of each edit)? What are my interviews saying? And how do I find supporting footage (re-enactments, b-roll, visuals) to highlight my topic or story?

Editing has helped me understand tremendously the immense value of getting adequate coverage material and shooting a master shot. Paying close attention to the lines of conversation, screen directions, lead room, head room, being able to see both eyes of a subject, cutting on the action...these various aspects all become vitally important when editing an entire sequence or a specific scene.

Non-linear or not, edit while you shoot.

TIP #2 - UNDERSTAND YOUR WORKFLOW

Understanding your workflow BEFORE you even shoot your project is critical. Where will this story play? What is the record format? The distribution specifications? Audio requirements? Aspect ratio? The list goes on.

Knowing how your project is going to flow (smoothly) through the post-production pipeline is just as important as knowing keyboard shortcuts and amazing editing effects. What are the codecs (compression-decompression)? How will you store media? What is your output & upload? Oh, better make sure your editor's software & hardware are compatible with the project. Having to convert to other formats costs time, energy...and money.

TIP #3 - GET ORGANIZED

Organization is incredibly helpful and important to your project.

As I started to tackle large, complex projects that took literally years to complete (with hundreds of videocassettes recorded), I learned the tremendous importance of shot lists, file numbering, listing best takes, tape and SD card numbering, knowing where everything was. I created separate bins with my best shots, interviews and cover footage.

Sure, there comes a point where one can be so organized that all creativity gets lost in the process, but really knowing your footage - both good and bad - is invaluable to your project. It will save you time, frustration and money...plus your sanity.

Remember to save and backup your project FREQUENTLY!

TIP #4 - THINK IN SEQUENCES

The great directors and producers - no matter fiction or non-fiction - know how to visualize, create and shoot whole sequences that tell their story. They see both the large picture, and the crucial shots necessary to complete that sequence. Edit meaningful sequences put in a coherent order, and you're half way to creating a larger story, segment, show, short film or documentary.

Ask yourself, what are the shots needed to shoot an entire scene? Opening, master, 2 shot, cut to over-the-shoulder, reactions, cutaways, traveling shots, close-ups, follow shots, coverage of action or dialog.

Don't think these shots have much to do with editing? They do.

Think in sequences.

TIP #5 - PAY ATTENTION TO NARRATION

Because good voice-over artists are usually expensive, I bring them to the project *after* the script has been finalized and approved by the client, myself, or both. Bringing these voice-over artists to participate at the end saves time and money, because having to re-book the narrator for pickup sessions - because the client (or you) keeps making word changes - accomplishes little else but frustration.

Until initial script approval, I record a temporary narration track (either myself or another reading the rough script) before recording FINAL narration. The editor and I first cut the project based on the rough narration, then we replace the rough track near the end with final voice-over, re-timing the edits based on the professional's pacing.

Which brings about a very critical objective: *Pick the right Narrator*. A great announcer makes your script better. Don't hire someone's brother-in-law or a disc jockey or a client's niece just because a higher-up thinks they have a good voice.

Go with a "pro" if at all possible. He or she will bring "life" to your script.

TIP #6 - MUSIC & SOUND ARE IMPORTANT

Music is critical to setting tempo & mood. Try really hard to pick the right tracks that match your visuals and project genre...or enlist a proper composer.

When financially possible, having a creative music composer is gold. In the past I've worked with Tim Hosman, who now creates network jingles and film soundtracks. Tim took my overseas sequences on the *Unreached People* documentary series and spun gold from straw. Again, don't hire a friend or someone's nephew just because they are a musician and can play a synthesizer. Soundtrack composing is a very specialized art form. Not everyone grasps the requirements of composing for video or film.

If you don't have the budget for a composer, then good, properly matched music tracks can make a difference as well. Music sets theme, emotion, style and feeling. There are plenty of great websites with reasonably priced theme music available for sampling and download.

Finally, *a good sound mix is critical.* Placing all the audio elements on individual tracks, then going the extra distance to mix down all your sound beds, separates the pros from the amateurs. Do a solid audio mix of music, narration, voices, effects & ambient sound to finish.

Your audience might tolerate sloppy video, but never sloppy audio.

TIP #7 - CREATE PROPER PACE & SPACE

Always consider your audience, message and the means of viewing. What is the best speed and timing to tell your story so it communicates to your viewer what you intend? There are dangers in editing a piece that's too fast...just as a project that moves too slowly puts people to sleep. Be sure to choose the right pace to tell your story effectively.

I'm a big believer in *substance* over *style*. Just because you possess a bag of editing tricks doesn't mean they are always correct for a specific clip, segment or sequence. Sometimes tricks are just...tricks.

Leave S-P-A-C-E. Let your pictures (visuals) and your sounds (audio) help carry your story.

Don't pack every moment on-screen with words (and music). Leave some *breathing room* so the viewer has time to consider narration and interviews. Introduce new pictures and sounds, then bring in voices.

TIP #8 - KILL YOUR DARLINGS!

Be willing to cut out your favorite scenes if it's necessary to further the story. Being willing and able to "kill your darlings" (as the old movie industry saying goes) is terribly critical to your project's success.

Yes, you may have loved that shot, interview or the extensive setup when you first filmed it - and probably argued intensely for the scene to remain in your project no matter the obvious. But if it's plain and clear that the terrific shot or shaky segment hinders your story, is too confusing or long, or just doesn't work on-screen...you *must* be willing to let it go.

Your story is your mission, right? *Nothing* is more important than your telling that story well; to bore (or confuse) people is the unpardonable sin of film, television and video.

TIP #9 - WALK AWAY

Go get some fresh air. Walk out of the edit suite. Eat lunch. Have some coffee. Sleep on it. Leave it for another day or tomorrow (if possible). Gaining a fresh perspective by walking away allows you to rethink a scene, shot or edit sequence. By coming back to the edit suite (or laptop) fresh, you often can improve the scene or segment.

Sometimes fatigue becomes one's own worst enemy. Too many mistakes are made because one is tired. Plus, when your eyes are glued to a computer or video screen for too many hours, one can lose valuable perspective and objectivity.

Walk away.

TIP #10 - SHOW YOUR PROJECT TO CIVILIANS

When your project is in good enough shape to show, try screening it for someone who's never seen it - but with the sound turned OFF. Pictures only. Ask the person afterwards what the story was about. If they can describe about 60-70% of the story (without sound), you're in good shape. The pictures are telling much (not all) of the story. If not, then your story might be too dependent on spoken content (voices).

Then, try showing your nearly finished edit to a *small* handful of people who are completely unfamiliar with your project. Hopefully, this group will match your intended audience. Stand at the back of the room with a note pad and pay close attention to their responses. If they're uneasy, bored or confused at certain parts, take note of those moments. Perhaps the pacing isn't right, or a section is too long, or there isn't enough supporting material. Maybe it's too many talking heads, or an interview is unclear.

They are seeing it for the *first* time, you for the *152nd* time. Their responses can prove invaluable. Pay attention to segments that work, too, making your audience cry or be transformed.

Finally, editing, to me, is immense fun. It's what re-writing is to writing - a chance to move things around, fine-tune, adjust, trim, layer, correct mistakes, replace, bring a segment to life.

But, your final edit is only as good as its ingredients - your production footage and elements. The better you conceive and shoot your project - with the final edit in mind - the more solid ingredients you'll possess when it's time to walk into the edit suite or over to the computer.

I will leave the rest of this chapter to the pros and their sage advice.

•

EDITING TACTICS FROM PROS

"Get it right the first time: Good photographer and sound man. Keep track of takes with notes."

- Mark Prest, sound mixer, Flat Tire Films

"When you are editing, the final master is Aristotle and his poetics. You might have a terrific episode, but if people are falling out because there are just too many elements in it, you have to begin to get rid of things."

- Ken Burns, legendary, award-winning filmmaker

"Editing is the hard, unglamorous part. Be as organized as possible. Descriptive file and directory names are lifesavers. Save your project regularly, mirror it to more than one storage device if possible.

"If you are making 'sub-masters' of any parts of your project - for export to *After Effects*, for example - save those in an uncompressed format. It will require a good amount of disk space, but will avoid the artifacting of concatenation (repeated compression) in the long run.

"Watch edited parts of it often, see how it 'feels' when you do. A well-edited piece should feel shorter than its actual running time. And be prepared to remove your favorite shot. You may be in love with the shot at the expense of the story.

"Have some 'civilians' watch the piece when it's nearing completion, and ask them how long they think it was. If they guesstimate shorter than the real running time, it's working. If they think it's longer, I know I have some more editing to do."

- Alan Lloyd, lighting cameraman

"Editing is when the real rubber hits the road. Screen EVERYTHING, organize it and log it. It feels like a huge mountain to climb at first, but it's funny how - once you know all of your footage - it comes into focus. You'll mentally start to eliminate all sorts of extra material and identify a lot of what you want to use to start with. String it together to tell your story. Don't worry about how long it is...yet.

"Now start to carve away WITHOUT MERCY. Less is more. Remember that the spoken word is great but you have motion and sound to tell the story as well. Use the best combinations of picture, sound, narration (if you are using it) and sound bites in the most efficient ways. Be ready to cut anything that doesn't propel your story forward with muscle and emotion. ANYTHING."

- Randy Martin, post-producer @ Atlas Media Group

"I find that audio editing is key, and rather unsung. I can tell if something is working by the sound of it, the rhythm, the energy. I would lay it out long in a 'radio' (audio only) cut, and then sculpt it...work with the pacing...then rough your pictures, then you start to edit."

- Kim Kennedy, coordinating producer, CBS News

"Always enter an editing room with a an editing script or at least a structure.

"Break your story into scenes and decide which scenes should follow others.

"Every shot or sequence should be motivated. Why is it there?

"Remember the story you are trying to tell and keep to the storyline. Once you veer off from it, you get in trouble.

"Remember you are editing a rough cut first. That means you don't agonize over every shot. Once you have a rough cut, you can polish it by changing shots and pacing.

"Most time in an editing suite is wasted arguing. Have your arguments before you go into the suite.

"If there is a dispute, don't let it last for more than fifteen minutes. You can either leave a black hole or do it one way or the other. Once you screen it, you will know which way works best.

"First, make the documentary that makes sense - then make it beautiful.

"Always, I repeat, ensure you know what you are trying to get the viewer to understand.

"You are not editing to show how clever you are, or to please yourself alone. It always must work for the people who will watch it.

"Highlight all your best shots - and if you can't get them in the first time around, try on the second edit.

"A shot doesn't only convey one idea. It can be used to say different ideas. So think of what else the shot can be used for. "

- Alan Mendelsohn, president, Just A Minute Words & Pictures

"Editing, is a little like directing a film after the fact - a good working relationship and communication between the Editor - Director - Producer is key!

"Always ask yourself 'is this shot moving the story forward?' and if it is...'is it moving the story forward too slowly?'

"If you are not engaging the viewer emotionally, then you're not really engaging the viewer at all.

"As far as emotional content goes, while a picture says a thousand words, I believe that sound and especially music convey emotion instantly - it's a universal language, Never underestimate the power of your soundtrack - for good or ill.

"Your audio can often carry 70% of the emotional content!

"From a technical point of view - sometimes compiling themed sequences is perfect when you need a little inspiration, and you can cut them down as you progress further. It can be far easier to find that missing shot(s) that will connect your narrative if you're looking at a sequence instead of a bin full of well labeled shots."

- Marcus Robb, creative director, Boogaloo Media

"The editor should be as passionate as anyone else involved in the film. They are the ones who bring together pieces to create as much emotion as possible. If it is meaningful to the editor, it will be meaningful to others. Editing with passion and emotion truly IS an art."

- Jaime Goldstein, Jacob Burns Film Center

"A good editor can save you from yourself (a bad one is like a root canal without anesthetic.) She/he sees only what is on the screen: it doesn't matter that you spent two days in the swamp waiting for the bad shot of the anaconda, had a passionate affair with a production assistant, or have great material that belongs in another film. The better your material, the more you need an editor to help you cut it; it is easy to dump inferior material - tougher when so much is good. The editor also acts as the voice of your public, getting you to clarify what is clear to you, but no one else."

- David Feingold, Ophidian Films

“Documentary art is a dance, a fluid movement, blending visual storytelling and the ancient oral tradition. Both elements create emotion. The rhythm of the work is born of this blending. (And yes, what joy when it feels like the piece has gone by ‘too’ quickly - a suspending of ‘time’.)

“What is your vision for undertaking this work? Keep this before you. Communicate it clearly to your team members. What discoveries have you made in the process of ‘capturing’ the images and the sound? What have the results in the field revealed to you? Which statements made by the essential characters and the sounds found in the location truly express the heart & soul of the piece?

“Return to the storyline often and have the courage to move elements of the story about. Use sequences to try out ideas. I truly believe that by paying very close attention to the ‘design’ and ‘gesture’ of each frame as they flicker across your eye and echo in your ear, you will move the work beautifully from rough cut to final. The sound must support the visual flow, measure by measure.”

- Bev Abplanalp, educator

“Editing is like the skill of writing for a writer, handling of the brush to a painter, the connection between conductor’s baton and an orchestra. Editing is the final stage of filmmaking where a film director uses the editor as a ‘tool’ to materialize his/her vision, and the editor has to be a sensitive and skillful artist that uses the director’s vision as a ‘tool.’”

- Erik Kapfer, exec producer, Film IT

“From the beginning, I still use a pin-board and index cards to physically move scenes on a wall. One scene per card with a quick title to explain what is being conveyed. I find it a great, inexpensive way to organize the show before the machines even get turned on. You will be surprised how many structural hurdles can be overcome this way!”

- Daniel Sheire, freelance producer/editor

"As a director, I worked for years with an excellent editor. We worked thus: We would screen all the rushes together. I would explain the storyline and the approach that I had in mind. I would go away until the editor had done his assembly. At that stage we would sit once more and start the serious business of fine-tuning. By leaving the editor to make the first cut we got his take on the footage. This was simply what is in the can, with no emotion about how hard it was to shoot or how difficult the subject was. It also gave me an alternative vision to the one that I had. The editing process can be the most rewarding and the most creative if you are working with an editor who contributes."

- Keith Hawke, Hawke Films

"I have had the good fortune to work with outstanding editors (and only one disaster). Working with editors is like love affairs: good ones are immensely pleasurable (though sometimes intense); rotten ones - get over them young, and at least you learn something from the experience. Also like love affairs, there is no one perfect formula that guarantees happiness for all.

"I like to sit and work through footage with my editor. I tend to do complex political documentaries. I certainly know more about the subjects than any editor I could hire. However, she/he represents the viewer; asks the questions that the viewer needs to know. A good editor can save you from yourself. He/she can help you tell your story more effectively and efficiently, while realizing your vision."

- David Feingold, Ophidian Films

"Before a single clip is uploaded it is essential that it's logged with as great a detail as possible. Taking good notes saves you time scrambling for that missing line/scene/shot later down the road. It doesn't matter if your film is 2 hours or 2 minutes - organization is the key.

"Also, having a good editor, who is more than a button pusher, is important. Collaboration can, and will, make your effort more gratifying - and perhaps this person may have an alternative idea that the producer/editor didn't think of.

"Stick with the story. Don't be afraid to put superfluous stuff on the cutting-room floor."

- Jeff Toback, producer, MLB.com

"Editors are very much like sculptors. They create a work of art from a lump of clay. It is an art - some would say a black art. Sound design and editing play huge roles in the editing process as well.

"I love editing: it's where the story comes together. When planning a shoot, writing the script, or on the set, I think like an editor, and how the material is going to work together. Being organized is critical to working smart and avoiding wasted time."

- Jon Leonoudakis, Evzone Media

"Focus helps you wade through material. Every scene should be about one thing, it should make one point and then you move on. Remove 'everything' that does not help you to make that one point."

- Nathan Shields, Freelance Picture Editor

"Editing is so all-consuming (particularly if you also shot the footage) that you need to allow time to walk away and shake it off, before the final few cuts. I'm always amazed at how easy it is, and how ruthless I am, when I return with fresh eyes, ears and heart."

- Simon Dikkenberg, producer, Siberg

"Breakup the editing with short breaks - go for a walk, etc. Relax your eyes so you do not strain them - looking away from the screen every 10 or 15 minutes helps a lot. Stay hydrated during editing, otherwise you get fatigued."

- Richard Sachs, GIA Film Productions

"Think of this: if in film there are three co-creators (scriptwriter, director and editor), documentary's co-creators would be: director, cameraman, and editor. What is shot, and what is shown, is as important as what you mean to say with it.

"I would recommend pre-viewings: When you need to show your film to someone not related to it, you realize immediately, what's necessary - and what's not."

- Sandra Rodriguez, director/screenwriter

"Editing is the best part of filmmaking. It's really where the film is made. I always have a general script to follow, and try to edit in the camera, as I'm shooting, if possible. I suggest you 'watch' your film while editing, as if you're the audience in the theater, not only the director and/or editor. Lose the ego, unless you've shot this film only for yourself & your mom to watch."

- Elizabeth English, Moondance Int'l Film Festival

"The most amazing scenes that work brilliantly alone, but end up slowing down/ruining the bigger picture/the film itself, they gotta go. Part of the job is to trust your instincts and develop a taste that reaches the audience you want to reach. And that should be instant, quick - and there's an art in having guts enough to trust those initial instincts."

- Merethe Rosvold, editor, GBFTE

"Editing is the best part of the whole process!

"Start by making a list of ten moments, shots, or pieces of sync that you cannot imagine not being in the film - having seen the rushes. Start with them. Do not get bogged down in extremely long rough cuts. It used to be how people did it, but with non-linear editing it really is not needed. Remember what these moments made you (and you hope the audience) feel.

"Doesn't matter if the film is 30 seconds long, or an hour and a half (I think most doc films beyond that are too long - as are quite a few of the shorter ones!). It is easy to get lost if you have a great deal of footage (I try and keep it down when I am shooting). Get these keystone moments in some kind of narrative order.

"See what this tells you. It is much easier to change the order at this stage than later.

"The film is nearly *never* the film you started out to make. Find the film in the rushes.

"Make sure that you start with something *dramatic* and 'in' the story (avoid worthy and over expositional starts), and climax and end with the most *dramatic* thing of all. Don't be afraid of using *humor* - it can work even in serious subjects if you are discerning.

“Make us care about the characters. Don't use too much exposition.

“Don’t fall in love with anything - structure is key!”

- David Pearson, producer-director, Arturi Films

CHAPTER 13 REVIEW: EDITING

1. Edit while you shoot.
2. Understand your workflow.
3. Get organized.
4. Think in sequences.
5. Pay attention to Narration.
6. Music and sound are important.
7. Create proper pace & s-p-a-c-e.
8. Kill your darlings.
9. Walk away.
10. Show your project to civilians.

CHAPTER 14: TIME MANAGEMENT

Never Enough Time

•

"I've had a wonderful time...but this wasn't it."

- *Groucho Marx, actor-comedian*

Time is one of the most valuable assets for your project or shoot. It's a commodity just as precious as money, talent, facilities, abilities and expertise. Use time wisely.

There's an old expression too often told that says, "never enough time to do it right, but always enough time to do it wrong."

Give yourself enough days and weeks (or months) to get the story right, with time well-spent recording the visual and sonic elements to tell it well, then create your best editing scheme to cut your piece with passion and quality.

I've found that far too many productions are in a rush, with rarely adequate time to shoot their film, video or documentary properly. Their projects seem to be constantly facing a time crunch. Requested footage was needed yesterday, or the video shoot was ordered on the quick, often because a producer waited far too late to make a final decision.

Sometimes this failure is due to "paralysis by analysis", where every single factor had to be weighed before mounting a shoot. Okay. But indecision remains a major factor too.

In the end, shooting as quickly as is humanly possible puts undue pressure on the project, and its people.

How many projects would've been saved with some more time?

•

MADRAS, INDIA

To this day I can still recall a by-the seat-of-your-pants shoot I did years back in India. It was for a really good group with high professional standards for broadcast television production. The trip resulted in two solid videos - one for fundraising that involved work at an orphanage, the other for inspiration and publicity promoting an upcoming citywide event.

The producer I was working with came from radio and had never managed or produced a video shoot before. And, unfortunately, this was my first - and only - project for the client. For I got into a small snit over the proper use of time management with the fledgling producer on the shoot, specifically for how the various interviews weren't being effectively planned and scheduled.

The breakdown started when the proposed four days for India production was reduced (for budgetary reasons) to three by the client. Try producing two full videos in just three days in busy, bustling "time has no meaning" Madras, India. Okay. We'll take the "get it done" approach.

But, from the start, the feeling for production felt like cramming way too much into the few hours or days scheduled. A "hurry-up" mentality was constantly being pushed. As cameraman, I felt like the lighting, sound and setups needed to be created quickly, for there were always going to be more on the producer's shot list to grab.

The orphanage footage and production was not difficult, for it all took place in a large multi-story building. The content was compelling, with a feeding ministry in place, plus the housing, clothing, schooling and care for hundreds of orphan children. There was also a wonderful medical clinic attached that served the poor and homeless with basic medicine and minor surgeries. The footage contained very worthy materials and stories. Since the location was confined to a single building, we were mostly productive each day.

However, one of the fiascoes in this arrangement of shooting two separate videos was that interviews for the second project were being setup on the fly. The card that was flipped is that interviews were taking place with just one person at their specific work place location across town based on their last minute, personal availability. Which meant that while we were effective at the orphanage, we'd have to jump into a car to drive miles away for an interview, setup, shoot, tear down, jump back into our car to return to the orphanage. These on-location shoots across town were causing us to lose precious time. If we'd arranged an entire afternoon or morning just for the interviews, we'd have done better.

It all came to a head on the last of our three days. Every objective that had not been shot on the producer's wish list now had to be recorded on that final day. Some interviews still hadn't been arranged or confirmed.

We started at 6 a.m. that morning, and still rolling, were headed to the last location at 7 p.m. that same night. I had a 1:50 a.m. flight to Greece, hadn't packed or showered, yet here I was headed to another cross town shoot on the last evening hours before leaving India for another assignment.

I spoke up to the producer while in the car to the last location. And my frustration showed. I grumbled that our rushing out to do these haphazard interviews could have been planned much better.

My speaking up didn't sit well with the young radio producer, who challenged me that maybe I just wasn't used to "working so hard and long." But, worse yet, my real point wasn't being understood - that our time as a production team wasn't being managed well.

That was the nail in my coffin for any future assignments: I had criticized the producer, who made sure to tell her bosses that I possessed, in her estimation, an "attitude" problem.

We were on completely separate pages.

She believed that no matter what she threw at me - even if it was her mistake - I was being paid, and that I should make it all work out.

My position was that she hadn't used our time properly, had crammed four days into three, and that everything we failed to shoot in the first two days was now being packed into Day 3.

To me, that was very poor planning and time management - even in India.

Time is either your best friend...or your worst enemy.

•

THE LUXURY OF TIME

Extra time will be a bonus when it rains on that important shoot day in the square, or an interview starts two hours late, using up an entire afternoon, not just a few hours. Adequate time to plan will allow a proper sound mix in post, a second fine cut for a segment, or a schedule for delivery of the final master that's not chaotic.

Production takes time, prep and editing too. It's all about smart, savvy time scheduling and project management - allowing yourself the time to do it right.

But too often when crunched, clients, producers, production managers or post supervisors will squeeze their deadlines (real or imagined) onto the project. Something has to give.

In the case of location shoots - especially overseas - production usually takes much longer than expected. The concept of time has a far different meaning in Latin America, Asia or Africa. Because time is treated uniquely in certain cultures, production teams need to learn how not to sweat the small stuff. Transport, meetings, appointments, traffic, goods, services and people - they rarely run efficiently to the beat of a metronome. Better make adjustments, and allow for the unexpected.

Frequently, I have jumped into a cab overseas, given the driver the address, negotiated the fare, then watched as the first place the taxi drove to was a nearby gas station. This unplanned fueling stop used up valuable travel time for me. But to the driver, his plan was to fill up his near empty tank only when his first paying passenger for the day arrived - me.

There is the production van that is supposed to arrive out in front of the hotel at 7:30 a.m. But, instead, pulls up at 8 or 8:30 a.m. The driver had to run an errand, or drop off the kids at school, then he headed to the hotel for the shoot. Ultimately, 7:30 a.m. meant one thing to you, another to him.

These are just two of many on-location examples I could give you. So, be adaptable, flexible and patient with time expectations when venturing outside your comfort zone. Consider giving yourself more time than you think. Because, invariably, you'll need that time.

Remember, creating some time on production shoots - when off duty - to have some fun with your team has tremendous benefits too. Producing a project is usually hard work, but also becomes a bonding experience, especially on the road. Everyone is thrown in together. Relationships form. Shared experiences - good, bad, funny, serious - bring people closer. So allowing a little time to have fun is a valuable tool. It shows to your staff and crew that they are worth it, which will come back to assist your project tremendously when a time crunch occurs or tension develops on the shoot. A little fun lets off steam.

Plan a great wrap party, or a special dinner out. Go to a famous site, take everyone to a memorable show or event in town. Your staff and crew will love it, and it will break the long tedious hours and monotony. Taking some time to have fun together speaks volumes to everyone on your project that they are valuable and important. Fun is a great tonic for team morale.

Finally, I would like to encourage you again to *find a way to get yourself organized.* Calendars, notebooks, dry erase boards, cell phone scheduling programs, appointment software, spiral ring notebooks or day by day journals...whatever works that keeps you on the right track, use it and live by it.

Creating a regular, daily list of things to do and prioritizing your time will prove beneficial for you...and your project.

Planning, writing, producing, directing, shooting, editing - spend your time wisely.

•

TIME TACTICS FROM PROS

"The saying goes, 'There is never enough time and money to do it right, but all the time and money in the world to do it over.' Take the time to do it right the first time. If that means spending a little more, it will be well worth its weight in time and money saved in the end."

- Dustin Ebsen, Beantown Productions

"I have never been anywhere outside the USA where time is as important as it is here. Just be prepared to wait...and enjoy this beautiful world while you're waiting!"

- Charley Buchanan, PBS cameraman

"Give yourself more time than you think."

- Steve Taylor, Digital Spatula

"Suggestions for shooting overseas: Someone on the crew needs to be experienced in overseas production. This can be the Cameraman, Writer or Producer.

"The more experience you have on your crew, the greater the chance of succeeding with your project.

"Expect everything to take twice as long overseas."

- Jim Rawn, Year 64 Media

CHAPTER 14 REVIEW: TIME MANAGEMENT

1. Time is either your best friend...or your worst enemy.
2. Time is one of the most valuable assets for your project.
3. Old Saying: Never enough time to do it right, but always enough time to do it wrong.
4. Don't become a slave to "paralysis by analysis."
5. How many projects would've been saved with some more time?
6. Be adaptable, flexible and patient with time expectations when venturing outside your comfort zone.
7. Creating some time on production shoots - when off duty - to have some fun with everyone has tremendous benefits.
8. Find a way to get yourself organized.

CHAPTER 15: TRAVEL & LOGISTICS

On the Road Again

•

"Travel is fatal to prejudice, bigotry,
and narrow-mindedness."
- Mark Twain, writer

AIRPORTS

Let's get serious. On Sept. 11, 2001, when four airplanes commanded by armed terrorists crashed into the *Twin Towers* in New York, *the Pentagon* in Washington, DC and a rural field in Pennsylvania, everything changed for air travel in North America and much of the world. Its ripple effect was felt elsewhere, too, at foreign airports and with international carriers across the globe.

Today, there is rarely, if ever, the chance to arrive at the airport at the very last minute. Easy security checks don't exist. Taking an extra carry-on is limited. Even checking a bag costs additional fees now. Meeting an arriving passenger at their gate has evaporated, for now you meet someone at the curb, or down at the baggage carousel.

What many Westerners didn't know, especially Americans, is that tighter restrictions and security in the world's airports had been going on for many years. In my experience, Israel is still the tightest, most restrictive country in the world. Better get to your airport (especially in Tel Aviv) four hours before your flight, for no one asks more detailed questions than Israeli security, and rightly so. Their viewpoint is that they are surrounded on three sides by enemies that wish to annihilate them; the fourth side represents their backs to the sea. They will make sure your travel story makes sense and that NOTHING is in your bag that might bring down an airplane or blow-up an airport. Period.

Travel has flown me through hundreds of airports across the world. It's been a myriad of endless jet ways, transit lounges and duty free kiosks. The big ones like Heathrow (London), Charles de Gaulle (Paris), Frankfurt Main, Schiphol (Amsterdam), Narita (Tokyo) and Changi (Singapore) are virtually cities unto themselves, with their own police forces, customs, immigration, hotels, restaurants and shopping centers. The same can be said for busy American airports in New York, Los Angeles (5th busiest in the world), Miami, Chicago, Atlanta, San Francisco, Denver, Dallas and Washington, DC.

Once you've dropped off the rental car, checked your mountain of luggage, paid the extra baggage charges, received boarding passes, cleared security, customs and passport control - you've finally made it, a process that might have taken hours.

So, congratulations. Enjoy the shopping. Grab a meal (hardly any served on the planes anymore), buy a book, walk the long terminals, listen to your iPod. Your long travel production journey - even for a short flight - is finally about to begin. You are going somewhere to shoot something important and interesting.

Travel well.

•

PLANES

It has gotten to the point that airplanes have truly become busses with wings. Some of the better airlines have become quite adept at providing creature comforts like in-flight videos and music to keep our minds entertained. Their goal is to have you back as both customer and passenger. But, to be real, it's become increasingly difficult to travel with any space or comfort anymore, whether short haul or long.

My experience is that the majority of flights I have taken are over oceans involving great distances. The average flight for me is perhaps nine to ten hours, so a quick trip to Phoenix at one hour or even Atlanta at five can be easily endured. But we've all missed connections, been delayed or found ourselves crammed next to someone who talks your head off or near the screaming baby with colic in the middle aisle.

Airplane travel is rarely, if ever, glamorous anymore. But the beauty is that a shiny tube of aluminum with engines called an airplane can fly you at 35,000 feet to new places on incredible adventures. If you view the journey as a chance to leave your comfort zone, to travel far and wide on a shoot with people who you respect and like, the travel process seems to take on a new meaning.

Most of my travel these days is in economy class, like many. One of the perks of traveling the world is a little known airfare I discovered years back called Around-The-World, also known as RTW. A number of the air alliances have them, Star Alliance being one of the best due to the number of routes and airlines available to make up one's own travel itinerary. One can circumnavigate the globe in either coach or business class (with up to fifteen stops) for about the same price as one would pay just from the USA to Europe and back sometimes.

I have used the RTW fare in Business class about a dozen times and the benefit (since I was often traveling alone as a one man band with 150 pounds of luggage) is that I got much better service, larger seats, better food and access to the airline lounges. But it comes with a very steep price, one that most productions are unwilling, understandably, to pay for in these days of shrinking budgets. However, when and if you have the budget, go for it, justify it when you can, because travel - especially international - will wreak extreme havoc on your body, mind and soul when you traverse across multiple time zones in just a few hours or days.

In economy class, prime seats, leg room and early boarding are the keys to success. Many times you can get your boarding pass online 24 hours before the flight now, or reserve your seats on an airline website at the time of booking. This is a great way to streamline your travel. It might also be possible - depending on your skills and the mood of the gate agent - to convince the airline for your crew to board with the premium class passengers, as I have often done just by telling the boarding gate agent that we are a camera crew that needs a little extra time to stow our bags and cameras.

•

TICKETING

AIRPORT: *Rule for the airline counter - ALWAYS try to be nice to the ticketing person and gate agents.* They have the omnipotent power to put you in the last row of the plane or divert your precious luggage to Bora Bora. Be nice, be patient, be sweet and try very hard to be kind. People handling ticketing get yelled at daily. As humans, they would much rather assist a NICE passenger than a RUDE one. *Honey catches more flies than vinegar.* Remember, they also have the power to upgrade you to that nice comfy seat in row 2.

WEB: There are some fabulous ways to save money on airfares these days, including dozens, if not hundreds, of discount web sites. I use *Tripadvisor.com* a lot to check what others say about a hotel. Airline web sites are often the best places to find a bargain with few booking fees. I also use *Expedia.com, Orbitz, Travelocity, LastMinuteTravel.com, CheapAirfare.com, Bing.com, Travelzoo.com* and others. The fun is in the hunt sometimes for the best fare at the best value. *But remember to keep the airport connections to a minimum for production travel.* Lost bags and airline delays make absolutely no sense on a shoot when time truly means money. Five stops at the lowest fare on an unreliable airline doesn't work. You saved nothing.

AGENCY: Even though there are some great web search engines out there, I also cannot overstate the importance of having a good, reliable and knowledgeable *travel agent*, especially if you have more than two to three crew members traveling together. A professional travel agent will pay for themselves in the extras they provide, especially if you are dealing with multiple itineraries and unfamiliar locations. Plus they know about deals you don't and, if their agency had been around for awhile, might offer special contract fares they've negotiated with the airlines.

Over the past few decades I've booked with Yeshoda (now retired) and Mary Jo at *MTS Travel* extensively. They've booked me on at least 1 million miles flown, having become a part of our team. Over many journeys and itineraries, they have come to understand the uniqueness of media production - including lodging, transportation and shoot requirements.

Good travel agents are worth gold. Find a good one, keep them, use them.

•

HOTELS

A big chunk of my working life has been spent staying in a room with a number on it: hotels and motels. I've stayed at a seedy hotel outside the Bombay airport next to rail tracks where the trains came running through every couple hours of the night.

During the Cold War, Moscow's old hotels required full payment BEFORE you took off from America and received your Russian tourist visa.

In Buenos Aires, the elevator stopped working, so we had to hand carry all our suitcases and gear down thirteen flights of stairs over numerous trips to make our cab to the airport.

A guest compound in the Congo was so overrun with large, flying cockroaches that I eventually came to expect these large, uninvited friends to be stowed in my carry-on luggage and crawling along the shower walls each morning.

If memory serves me correctly, the toilet paper in Havana's *Riviera Hotel* is so rough that you could sand wood with it.

Experience has taught me that the hotel rooms in Europe are usually small with plumbing fixtures truly unique. That Asia has incredible customer service for Westerners. That you can find a *Marriott*, *Sheraton*, *Hilton*, *Hyatt*, *Accor* or *Best Western* in most any medium to large, civilized city anywhere in the world.

The nicest room I have ever stayed in was the presidential suite at the *Hyatt Regency* in Singapore. My cameraman, Jimmy, and I were upgraded because the hotel was fully booked when we arrived at 2 a.m. from a long Japan flight. The vast suite had just about everything: an office, full kitchen, three bathrooms, two bedrooms, a television in the sauna, dining area and living room. It would have been quite easy to just move in and live. The suite had most recently been used by the Sultan of Brunei. You and I will hardly ever stay in such suites.

With little argument, the undeniably worst room I have ever stayed in was a terrible, ramshackle motel in Ngozi, Burundi, East Africa. The bathroom was crude and had not been cleaned, the towels still smelled of the previous occupant's sweat, and the soiled sheets had not been changed. To top that off, there was no hot water. When I took my long anticipated shower - after two days upcountry without bathing - flying termites swirled at my feet and a rodent stuck its head through the broken bathroom window to see what I was doing. To add insult to injury, I broke a tooth on a tough chicken dinner a few hours later in the café. It was a truly remarkable, memorable experience, but never again.

My point in sharing these little anecdotes is that you will have great hotels - and shabby ones - along the way. What you try to aim for is something in-between based on budget, comfort and location. Try to find a good, clean, safe and reasonably priced hotel that fits what the project can afford. It doesn't have to always be modern - for the quaint, charming hotel with character can be wonderfully memorable too, as long as they've dusted.

Another important factor is to try and put everyone in your team in the SAME HOTEL. This may not always be possible due to the size of your production group and the unique logistics in a city or country, but most teams are two to five people. Keep them in the same hotel or motel if at all possible for practical reasons.

For our *PBS* shoot in Paris years back, the crew were housed in two different hotels in separate, distant parts of the city because the producer had made special deals with the hotel operator/packager, a barter arrangement that saved the TV program travel money. The downside was that our production easily lost up to two good hours of available light each day just picking up people and dropping them off in packed Paris traffic. Those lost hours were valuable moments wasted that could have been used shooting extra footage with more setups along the way - if everyone has just been in housed in the same hotel.

Never be penny wise, but pound foolish.

Remember this: a good hotel room is your home away from home. It's where one sleeps, showers, works, talks, eats, puts in laundry, checks messages and relaxes at the pool or goes to the gym. The quality standards of the hotel reflect what your management team thinks of their staff, crew and, sometimes, the talent.

In the grand scheme of things, do your research, read recommendations, crunch the numbers and **pick the best hotel your budget can afford.**

•

TRAVEL MONEY

Cash (ATM) machines, debit/credit cards and electronic banking have made the money factor of traveling for production easier than ever. Whether to another state, province or across the world, gone is the day when producers or production managers would need to carry piles of travelers checks on them, though some still do.

Transferring money into accounts can be done easily now by computer, fax or even mobile phones. Tracking expenses via web or smart phone makes staying on-budget easier. My only suggestions for money management for travel are these:

ATM/CASH MACHINES: Upon arrival in another country try to find a local ATM machine and pull out an adequate amount of the local currency to get your team into town or to cover expenses for the first few days. Check with your own bank to see what other banks they partner with in your state or country of production and try to use these affiliate banks if possible. Doing so will often cut down on additional transaction fees.

USE BANKS: Stay away from the currency exchange counters, especially at the airports or train stations. Their rates are unfavorable and they also make hidden money with the "transaction fee." Instead, go into a reputable bank during the daylight hours that changes money. Or, as mentioned, use the ATM, as the fees are nominal and the exchange rate is the most current. Try to pull out a good chunk of cash at a time to keep the nominal transaction fees to a minimum.

PREPAID PHONE: Sometimes buying a local prepaid phone in the location country is cheaper than using your own personal cell phone. For $50-$100 you will have a regional phone that makes calls in-country for pennies per minute, not dollars. Let everyone in your crew, the local contacts and even those back home know what this new phone number is. If you are dealing with a phone that has menus in another language, have the phone salesperson help you with the setup before you leave the store. Try to buy a prepaid card for future calling too.

NOTIFY YOUR HOME BANK & CREDIT CARD COMPANY YOU ARE TRAVELING: Call, contact or email your local bank and credit card providers before you travel outside the country to let them know in advance where you're going to be, what kind of charges you might be incurring and when you will be returning. That way the card issuers will not freeze your credit while they try to figure out why there are charges coming in from Brazil (while you're shooting in Rio). Just a few phone calls before you leave as a courtesy to your banks makes a huge difference, saving you frustration and embarrassment.

CASH: Cash is still king. Despite the multitude of places that take Visa and MasterCard, cash - especially in small notes and denominations - is needed and necessary, especially for small, minor expenses. Remember to only carry as much local currency that you believe you'll need for the day, nothing more.

HIGH LIMIT CARDS: When checking into a hotel or renting a car or van, try to use the credit card with the highest available balance, especially if you own an American Express card, which - in theory - has no spending limit. Hotels and car rental agencies block out big chunks of money on credit cards so that if a customer skips on the bill, the agency or hotel is covered for the spending to date and any potential losses. Use your Visa and MasterCard for the meals and getting around - Amex or Diners Club for hotels and rentals.

COPIES OF CREDIT CARDS: Make photocopies or scans of your credit cards and list the correct phone numbers too. Keep these separate from the cards themselves. If you're robbed or lose a credit card you will have the necessary account numbers available to report the loss and cancel the specific card. Consider enrolling in an identity theft or credit card protection service. By calling just one number and reporting the loss, they will do the contacting for you.

RECEIPTS: Keep all your receipts. Write down what you're spending. Over the years I have used 6" by 9" clasp envelopes for all my spending, writing on the outside what each numbered or lettered receipt was for, the amount in local currency and the exchange rate at the time of the transaction. I try to keep up with my expenses for the production daily, regularly, so they don't pile up. For cash transactions like tips or out of pocket, I write on the envelope the initials NR, "no receipt." Keeping up with your expenses in a timely manner will help you tremendously if you are required to complete a detailed travel report later for clients or employers.

•

MEALS

Your meals for production can vary from catered dinners at the studio to ordering off the local menus at the edit suite. An army, they say, marches on its stomach, so food is important to not only the team's strength, energy and nutrition, but its morale too. How you feed your production people, staff and workers says a lot about how you value them, or not. Time and again, when the food is good, the crew will not only brag about the meals and you, but will often go the extra mile to work harder for you when the project goes into overtime or everyone is stressed. Get *cheap* on them, they will get *expensive* on you by finding "creative" ways to add little billable items to their invoices somehow.

In my case, I am the luckiest person in the world with the many sumptuous meals eaten across the world. Peking duck at the Peking Hotel in Peking. Couscous in Paris. Chinese food in Rome. Wild boar in Croatia. Chicken feet in Macao. Paella in Madrid. Gaucho steaks in

Buenos Aires. Japanese breakfast in Nagano, Japan. Huevos Divorciados in Saltillo, Mexico. Avocado salad in Ayacucho, Peru. Sushi in Oslo. Injera in Addis Ababa. King Klip fish in Capetown. Roasted goose in Budapest. Indian tandoori in Nairobi. Greek pitas in London. You get the idea.

The incredibly long list of great, memorable meals across the globe is still etched in my mind, including the settings, tastes and great people I sat, talked and consumed with. I don't see food just as "fuel." In the end, the shoots were great, but the people and meals made them even more special. Seeing the world, shooting in so many cultures provides the opportunity to order unique, tasty foods from their national cuisine. My suggestion is to enjoy, try something new, get out there and experience what the local country and cuisines offer you. Don't always be stuck to the hotel or motel due to the convenience. You can always have McDonalds at home or Starbucks, but Turkish coffee in Sarajevo will be a drink you'll remember forever.

Finally, remember how mom told you that breakfast was the most important meal of the day? She was right. Especially during production or traveling, breakfast is often the only meal you can count on. All other meals are up for grabs. When out of town or overseas, get to the coffee shop or café early to eat a good, filling breakfast. Concentrate on the protein, not the breads and carbs, which burn off quickly. Your morning meal might need to hold you over till lunch at 1 or 2 p.m. (or even later). Bring snack or nutrition bars along to tide you over too.

And, of course, bring some Imodium, Pepto Bismol, Rolaids and Tums with you.

•

TRANSPORT

During my career, I have traveled by jumbo jet, prop plane, small airplane, helicopter, rickshaw, row boat, ferry boat, propeller boat, dug out canoe, train, camel, horseback, truck, bus, passenger van, car and taxi. How you chose to get your team around is up to your budget, destination, schedules, the logistics at hand, time constraints, and the size of your gear and luggage.

TAXIS: Whenever I can, I try to rely on the client or host to have their local contacts or representatives arrange the transportation, including drivers. This usually works out well, as long as the vans or minibuses are large enough. But many times overseas if I am traveling alone, or with a cameraman, my experience has been to hire taxis. Whenever possible, determine the price in ADVANCE. Or get an estimate. No one needs to be arguing over cost once you hit the final destination. If sitting in the back seat, sit opposite of the driver so he (or occasionally she) can turn and get directions from you. Make sure they can also see you in their rearview mirror.

Getting around like this requires having a workable plan with your team for entrance and exit. I try to pay the driver while still in the cab. Why? Once I get out and start to pull money from my pocket I become vulnerable to those on the street passing by. There is no use in your becoming a prime target for petty theft or predetermined distractions. By staying in the cab, I am usually only dealing with one person: the driver.

My good buddy, and former cameraman, Jimmy Hodson, and I had a great routine for many years and across 5 continents. He would start pulling out the gear from the taxi while I paid. Jimmy is 6'8". No one messed with him (or the gear). We did splendid with this routine in more than 30+ countries and scores of shoots.

When I find a good, reliable taxi driver, I often will hire him for the rest of my time in that city or town. I will negotiate a flat rate per day with him, sometimes including the final trip to the train station or airport to drop us off. Plus, I will make sure to get his business card with his cell number, so I can call in advance to arrange time and place of pickup. I've even had the taxi agree to drop us for dinner and return at a set time for the ride back to the hotel.

Hiring the taxi outright is often cheaper than trying to hail taxis as we go, which can be hit or miss. Having our own taxi is far more efficient and predictable. That way we can hop out to grab shots of the monument or traffic circle, then jump back into our waiting taxi.

By keeping the same cab, the process is streamlined. And you can learn valuable information from cab drivers, for they are excellent gatekeepers of news, information and advice about their city, much of it humorous. Plus, they will know where many of the best eating establishments are. You can't underestimate that for a hungry crew.

All in all, I've been very successful at this buy out arrangement, the only trouble coming is when a taxi driver doesn't have a meter or is dishonest in his approach, shaving the truth on costs or final fees. When that happens, all bets are off, so we find another taxi.

And, always beware of the phrase "no problem."

NAV SYSTEMS: If you do rent a car or van, especially in North America or Europe, opt for the extra navigator system available at the rental counter. Simply by typing in the addresses of your destinations, the nav system will guide you, saving you time and frustration. If possible, and the budget permits, secure a driver who knows the local roads and conditions. This will take the stress out of having to drive so you can relax and concentrate on your shoot. Letting someone else who is knowledgeable do the driving is using your time and resources very wisely.

HOTEL BROCHURE: If you are in a country where your own language is not the primary language, or you're not familiar with your location, take a hotel brochure or business card with you. Make sure to have the front desk person or a concierge write on the back where the hotel is in the main *language* and *alphabet*, including specific directions, the right neighborhood, major landmarks. I found out while in Hong Kong that this was vital as many drivers only read Cantonese. Simply handing them the hotel card in Cantonese got me back to my hotel (the New Astor) more quickly and efficiently every time.

•

IRAQ BORDER

On the lonely, northern territory between Silopi, Turkey and Sakhu, Iraq is a dusty border crossing that straddles the mighty Tigris River. It is a small outpost with big oil tanker trucks lined up for miles on the Turkish side ready to cross the border into Iraq, fill their empty tanks with cheap fuel, then turnaround and return to Turkey to sell for a huge profit.

It was at this border in June, 2003 that I stood with three Turkish friends. This was just a couple months after the American military had taken control (whatever that term means) of Iraq, ousting Saddam Hussein from power. Our assignment was to travel through Northern Iraq meeting with churches and non-profit groups so as to establish working relationships for further humanitarian aid and assistance. My job was to document the trip on video for a possible fundraising segment for my U.S.-based client.

My new colleagues were stopped, questioned and held up for overnight by the Turkish officials to determine their true purpose for entering Iraq during such a volatile period. They were also questioned because they were Turkish Christians, a very tiny minority (less than 1%) to Turkey's predominantly Muslim majority.

After their motives were explained and their traveling documents were cleared the next morning, we drove 200 meters over the Tigris to the Iraqi side of the border. Being an American, I had very little trouble crossing into Iraq, only needing to show my US passport to an American solder at that time, a visa not even necessary. At that important moment of entering Iraq, it was a young sergeant who struck up a casual conversation with me that provided the best safety advice anyone could have given us. The soldier asked where we were going, to which I replied that perhaps we'd make it as far as Baghdad. He cautioned not to do so, that driving the more than 300 miles south to the capital city on the only highway would result in our van being stopped by bandits, then robbed.

The other nugget of advice he offered was also golden. He strongly suggested that we not drive around in our Turkish van, because Iraqis would see we were from a richer country and would not only rob us, but perhaps shoot at us too. Change out our van, he told us.

When we arrived in the city of Dohok, a mid-sized city perhaps 50 miles inside the border, we hired a local Iraqi driver who owned an older Chrysler mini-van with Iraqi plates. We left the Turkish van at our hotel, paid local security to watch it, then traveled everywhere with our newly hired Iraqi driver guiding us.

This turned out to be a very smart move, for the driver knew the Iraqi roads and their conditions well, including where fighting was still going on (in Mosul). But because we were in an Iraqi van with local license plates, we were rarely stopped, despite the fact that the occupants were three Turks and an American with a TV camera.

The American sergeant and his sage advice at the border truly saved us - and the trip. Plus, hiring the local Iraqi driver with his own air-conditioned van was a shrewd tactic too.

The moral of this little war story is to use good, reliable local people in your shoots and travels, for they are worth gold. They know the lay of the land, can provide insider information, and will steer you, hopefully, out of trouble time and again.

•

TRAVEL DOCUMENTS

My primary job as a department head on Season 14 of *The Amazing Race* for *CBS Network* was for my assistant, Maria, and I to coordinate and make sure that every single passport, foreign visa and country work permit was squared away for about 105 potential travelers. These included senior network vice-presidents, advertisers, executives, producers, crew, production coordinators, couriers...and contestants. We had crew from across the world, handling personnel from Canada, UK, Argentina, Brazil, Israel, South Africa, Italy, New Zealand, Holland, Mexico and Trinidad.

For a show of that size - with so much at stake - it was a mammoth task that took sixteen weeks of prep before *Start of Race*, then constant vigilance while *The Race* was crossing time zones and landing in hot spots on three continents. We learned to be thorough, detail-oriented, organized and meticulous. Strong people and communication skills came into play virtually every day too, including working and negotiating with foreign embassies where *The*

Race would stop. Here are just a few tips that will help your next shoot, whether a country away, or on the backside of the world:

DRIVER'S LICENSE: Bring it. You may need to rent a car. But if you aren't driving that day, leave it in the hotel or room safe. It's an important piece of identification and difficult to replace should you lose it. Got a AAA auto club card? Bring that too, for AAA has great member benefits across the world, including hotel and car discounts. You may need to apply for an *International Driver's License*. Check with your local Auto Club for information. And, no, I don't work for AAA...but I should. Their membership has incredible value for the small fee paid.

PASSPORTS: Don't have one? Get one right away. I have a talented producer friend who kept missing possible production trips to Europe because he simply didn't possess a passport. No passport, no trip. In the USA, there are tons of post offices that can facilitate your application. Do a web search for the nearest to you, fill out the app, get some passport photos (any good xerox or photo place can take your picture) and pay the fee. If this is your first passport, you will need to bring an ORIGINAL birth certificate with you to start the process. For renewals, bring your most recent passport.

Need a passport or its renewal quickly? I use *Travel Document Systems* in Washington, DC for the East Coast and *Ambassador Passport and Visa* in Santa Monica, CA for West Coast. They can obtain a passport or a renewal for you in as little as 24-48 hours - or even same day. An expedite is one to two weeks. You will need to provide a travel itinerary showing you are leaving overseas soon.

Occasionally, check your passport for its expiration date. In the USA they are good for ten years, children and teenagers for five years. If you travel extensively, check to see how many available blank pages you have, for some countries will only give visas if two facing pages are clear for stamping.

WORK PERMITS: Many countries require a business visa or a local work permit to do shoots in their country. Web searches will help you there. So will the official film commissions of countries, cities, provinces and territories where you'll be shooting. Their representatives are there to help and assist you. Contact them and ask. No question, even if considered simple, is off limits. They want to encourage your bringing production to their region or locale.

VACCINATIONS: Yellow Fever is good for ten years. Virtually any developing country (especially in Africa) will require it. Tetanus is also necessary. Hepatitis shots are also a very good idea in this day and age. Ask your local health clinic, tropical medicine doctor or your HMO for their advice. Getting your vaccinations well in advance will put less pressure on your trip. And remember that a scheduled series of booster shots are often necessary for some vaccines. Malaria is a series of pills taken the same day each week starting BEFORE your trip commences. So, keep to the schedule, even after returning!

If your client, or the production, will cover vaccinations within their budget, good, because immunizations can be very expensive. However, if you shoot overseas frequently, you may need to cover the cost of these fees yourself and to keep your vaccinations up-to-date simply as the "cost of doing business."

•

WHEN SICKNESS STRIKES

Across over 100 overseas trips, both for work and pleasure, I have been sick three times. Morocco was the worse, with severe dehydration, upset stomach and the runs. I lost seven pounds in just five days the hard way.

In Ethiopia, I drank from a dirty, contaminated water glass at a Chinese restaurant in Addis Ababa. Next day was spent sick in bed, ashen-faced and without strength. With the help of a great producer, Jeff Evans, I got back to California, finally gathering strength closer to home on a final flight from New York to San Francisco.

A dirty hotel air conditioner in a seedy hotel dump in Nagpur, India also landed me into bed with a virus for a few days. The client had guessed at where to house the group, and ended up trying to save money. Moral of that story: whenever possible, book a reliable hotel with good food and clean rooms.

Knock on wood, across almost 2 million air miles and about 4 years of my life traveling, working and shooting overseas I've been pretty fortunate at staying healthy.

MEDICAL INSURANCE: There have been many times on what I considered dangerous trips that I contracted with an international medical insurance company - *Wallach & Company* - to cover my travels. For just about $5 a day I am insured against medical emergencies, even if an airlift to a nearby country for critical attention if necessary. Travel medical insurance is money well-spent.

EMBASSIES: Have your production team research the appropriate embassies where your shoot will take place. Notify embassy officials when you are in-country that you have arrived, plus inform them how long your team will be staying and where. I have found that an embassy is chock full of good, practical information that can help your production and team. Plus they know nearby contacts and resources should an emergency arise. (And the Marines will often show you a good time.)

May your health always be good. But should something happen, get to a doctor or head to the best, closest hospital or clinic at the very first sign of trouble.

•

TRAVEL ADVICE BY THE NUMBERS

1. When you are on a project out of town or on the back side of the world, **take precautions**. Watch out for your team, from lowest to highest on the totem pole. Be careful of risks, both internal (food, viruses) and external (security, safety).

2. **Know where your room is in the hotel** and how to evacuate quickly if necessary.

3. Write down the **room numbers of other crew** on a pad of paper next to your phone.

4. **Keep track of each other**, especially if someone wanders off to sight see and doesn't return at a normal time or hour. This

includes the migrating crew member at the airport who loses track of the time and proper gate for your next flight.

5. **Be careful what you leave in your rooms** and especially the production vehicle. Meet and talk to the head of hotel security if it's possible to lock your gear in a safer location.

6. **Only carry as much money as you need for the day.** Leave the rest in the hotel or room safe for security reasons.

7. Use **money belts** or sleeves that go around your waist, arm, neck or leg to secure your valuables. Carry the bare basics of currency and a credit card in a front pocket close to you.

8. If possible, try to **carry only a copy of your passport** and the appropriate country visa with you on the streets, leaving your original passport back in a room or hotel safe. This may not always be possible or practical in a country where a physical passport might be required to be carried physically for identity reasons, especially in developing countries. But if *copies* will do, take them instead. (I have had two passports stolen from me on the streets of Buenos Aires and Casablanca. Nothing stings like a lost passport.)

9. Leave the expensive watch and the dazzling jewelry at home. **Only wear what you would be willing to lose**.

10. For equipment bonding **carnets**, take the document in your carry-on luggage.

11. **Scan a copy of your current passport and e-mail it to yourself**. Leave it in a folder on your e-mail provider or on a flash/ thumb drive. That way if you ever lose your passport you can go to any internet café or hotel business center and print a copy of your passport as proof of your citizenship.

12. **Make four to five photo copies of your passport**. Put individual copies in each of your carry-on and checked bags.

13. Bring three to four **extra passport photos** with you, just in case. They are great for getting visas on the road or for an application should you lose your passport.

14. Create an **itinerary** with key dates, places, contact details, addresses, hotels, flights etc. Give copies to every important person in your life. Put extra copies in your carry-on bags. Make sure to include your itinerary in your checked bags. That way airline baggage personnel can find you when they open your lost or delayed luggage.

15. Whenever possible, **check in as a group** at the airline ticket counter - that way you can pool your baggage allowances.

16. If you have a long layover in an airport, consider a **day pass** into one of the executive lounges. The minimal cost is well worth the sense of privacy and calm. These lounges also have dedicated ticketing counters where you can arrange for boarding passes and get flight updates. Many have showers!

17. Should you have more than six to eight hours between flights, book a **"Day Room"** at a nearby airport or terminal hotel. The chance to sleep, shower and refresh yourself will make a huge difference in energy, rest and morale.

18. **Melatonin!** This natural herbal pill, available at most any drug store, helps the body relax and adjust to new time zones by aiding your sleep pattern. Take before going to sleep over the first few nights of your trip. It makes a world of difference for jet lag.

19. **Drink lots of water.** On the plane, take sips, so that your bathroom breaks will be kept to a minimum. Throughout your time in production, keep hydrated.

20. On **long plane flights**, I bring an eye mask, ear plugs and change into my sweats for sleeping. The mask cuts out distracting light, the plugs reduce noise, and I sleep more comfortably in the loose sweats. Before arrival, I change back into my street clothes.

21. In developing countries - or anywhere you don't trust the tap water - **use bottled water to brush your teeth.**

•

TRAVEL TACTICS FROM PROS

"For travel to developing countries consider these rules:

"RULE #1 - **Do not expect a productive first day upon arrival**. As a matter of fact, the first few days often find a crew struggling to adapt to the new time zones. For overseas shoots, in most cases a crew is traveling thousands of miles in two or three days. If you've traveled economy class then most likely your crew will be a little stiff and tired.

"RULE #2 - **Always arrange for large vehicles that can handle a lot of luggage, equipment and people**. Once you've passed through customs, the true journey begins. To start that journey, vehicles that can handle all the luggage and equipment need to be ready.

"Cramming ten people into one caravan is not a recommended practice. Video and Audio equipment need special handling. I always recommend one vehicle for the crew and their equipment, plus another for all remaining travelers. The last thing you need is a suitcase squeezing your backup camera and snapping a lens off. Once you arrive, treat your crew's equipment as if it's the ONLY thing that matters.

"RULE #3 - **Getting a good first night's sleep is crucial**. For that reason, if possible, put the crew up in a better hotel. One that has clean rooms, running hot and cold water, a restaurant, security and a business center. Jet lag needs to be slept off...don't hit the ground and start running immediately.

"RULE #4 - **Time is money....do you want to be shooting or sitting in a car?** The daily costs of a crew make it imperative to maximize their time on the ground. For that reason, if the final location for shooting is more than a couple hours away, then internal flights should be considered. Consider charters if they'll save you time. Once you arrive in the community chosen for shooting, the daily logistics need to come into play. Again, you don't want to be driving two hours into the community and two hours out each day.

"RULE #5 - **Find a good local hotel** that can serve basic food, has locked doors, screened windows, bathrooms and, if possible, air conditioning.

"RULE #6 - **Try to be as inconspicuous as possible**. Inevitably a camera crew draws attention. For that reason, it's imperative that you have the support of the local people. In a perfect world you should be able to shoot with some local support for crowd control. A shooting day needs to include travel to and from multiple locations. You need to plan ahead and be prepared for unforeseen interruptions."

- Jim Rawn, Year 64 Media

"Make sure you have your *tripod plate* with you. It's almost impossible to get one overseas if you forget it. In fact, keep an extra one in your bag at all times.

"Borrow/rent extra batteries for trips overseas. You never know if you'll be in a position to charge up when you need to.

"Take your camera on the plane when possible. Don't depend on the airlines to take care of your number one asset.

"If you're shooting on memory cards, backup to external portable hard drives on-location. They are cheap compared to re-shooting.

"Pull you selects (good shots) from the footage during your down time if you have a computer with you. This will save you a ton of time later. You can even do a quick montage of shots for the client, who will love that kind of peek."

- Steve Taylor, Digital Spatula

"Tip - Always check with your airline to see if they have the space for your gear...not just going but coming back as well!!!"

- Dana Millikin, network producer-director

"It's always good to be flexible and think outside of the box when purchasing tickets. You won't always get the best price from a travel agent. Don't be scared to do some research and find cheaper fares online but at the same time understand the fare rules of the tickets you are purchasing. Understand that as a production you have buying power, so get in contact with airlines and make deals. You would be surprised at how many airlines are very eager to work with productions and will negotiate really good deals in exchange for a promotional mention, etc.

- Juree Rambo, World Race Productions

CHAPTER 15 REVIEW: TRAVEL & LOGISTICS

1. It has gotten to the point that airplanes have truly become busses with wings.
2. Rule for the airline counter - ALWAYS try to be nice to the ticketing person and gate agent.
3. Remember to keep the airport connections to a minimum for production travel.
4. Good travel agents are worth gold. Find a good one, keep them, use them.
5. Never be penny wise, but pound foolish.
6. Pick the best hotel your budget can afford.
7. A production crew marches on its stomach.
8. Beware of the phrase, "no problem."

CHAPTER 16: RESPECTING OTHER CULTURES

Cultural Differences

•

"What we've got here is failure to communicate."

- Strother Martin, the Captain

(Cool Hand Luke, 1967)

Over the course of directing numerous film and television projects, video segments and documentaries across the world, I have worked and engaged with literally scores of diverse peoples and cultures. Traveling and shooting on-assignment has brought me in touch with dozens of language groups, spiritual beliefs and ethnic make ups. Naturally, I have not come out unscathed, for I have made more than my fair share of terrible and embarrassing stumbles. A few of these awkward cultural mistakes remain permanently tattooed into my human psyche.

NIGER: Once, in the fiercely hot, dusty West African city of Niamey, I accidentally tripped and fell over a Muslim child's dirt mound grave covering an outdoor funeral ceremony. The Imam and family conducting a nearby burial service were both incensed and irate at my trespass. They shouted, shook their fists angrily and threatened to tear me apart, for I had desecrated an infant's grave site. I didn't blame them then for their anger, or now. As humbly, and as respectfully, as I could muster, I apologized profusely and repeatedly...then quietly escaped with my life. Dignity be damned. You dust yourself off, say you're sorry, then get out of there quickly.

MOROCCO: Finishing up a sprawling gardens, pool and architecture segment at the luxurious *La Mamounia Hotel* in Marrakech, I had struck up, what I perceived, as a chatty rapport with the attractive female guest services guide. She had arranged the location shoot and entrance into the hotel's exquisite suites and sumptuous rooms. Just as I was packing gear, and in a far too nonchalant manner, I bent to kiss her hand. Stunned, she quickly pulled back her hand, curtly escorted me to the lobby, then turned and walked back hurriedly to her marketing office. Being a young Moroccan woman, she viewed my casual French-type gesture as rude, sexual and an insult. My lame attempt at a debonair, European hand kiss had truly offended her. Considering my actions, what was I thinking? She was right, I was wrong, and I tried with great effort both to apologize and make amends. But the serious damage was already done and finished. So was the shoot.

INDIA: While shooting footage on the Ganges River in Varanasi, I noticed just outside the nearby temples that dead bodies were being burned in holy Hindu burial ceremonies. My inner voice reminded me that my production client back in the USA had *strongly* urged me to record whatever funeral pyres I might find on my assignment along the Ganges. But another voice speaking to me echoed from the young Indian man who was rowing his crude wooden boat down the river, my being his client. Previously, he had warned that the fiery funeral rites on the banks were considered off limits and sacred according to his Hindu faith.

Despite his sincere warnings, I turned and quickly shot some video footage of a burning body just as we floated by a burning pyre. The boat owner was not pleased. And I knew, and sensed, that my casual actions had truly offended his Hindu beliefs, for his facial expressions changed from pleasant to intense during our ride down the river. Pleasing my Western clients was little solace for the inner spiritual anger I had caused the boat owner with my shooting in the wrong direction at the wrong time.

•

GETTING IT RIGHT

In my numerous overseas travels, I could conjure up many more embarrassing moments, but these three particular miscues will do. Stepping in the wrong pile of mess has not always been the case, for I have been respectful and sensitive during other cross cultural challenges along the way too.

CAMBODIA: At the horrific *Killing Fields*, just outside Phnom Penh, are deep, dug out lime pits where people young and old were slaughtered and decapitated with sharp shovels by the brutal Khmer Rouge. Severed heads often went into one pit, bodies into another. Their bloody skulls were later stacked at a nearby monument on the grounds dedicated to the fallen and forgotten killed along the Mekong River. Before even pulling out my camera to start recording, I chose to walk the site quietly, and prayerfully, first. Taking time to observe these hallowed, haunting grounds, and to consider this tragic holocaust for the genocide that it was, became my way of respecting and honoring the deaths of the millions of innocent lives that had perished there. When the proper time had passed, only then did I began shooting video footage.

UGANDA: In Kampala, my very good friend, field producer and colleague, Greg Fisher, took me on a survey visit to an AIDS hospital in the heart of the capital city. The facility was packed with the near dead and dying, all of whom were required during their medical stay to rely on their immediate families and friends for their basic food, clothing, bed sheets and cost of medicine. Greg and I somberly walked the dark hallways, going from bed to bed, room to room. We smiled at the patients, nodded our heads in quiet acknowledgment, but said little, if nothing, throughout our walk. Finally, after we had explored most of the hospital, I pulled Greg aside and told him that I just didn't feel it was right to record footage. It was a place of death. The dying, I believed, should have their dignity and respect - which, to me, included the right not to have an expensive video camera pointed at their misery.

THAILAND: Outside Chiang Mai, I was assigned to cover a caring Christian orphanage that assisted Thai children and infants afflicted with AIDS. These little ones, some of them newborns, had contracted the disease from their mothers, or through tainted blood transfusions. In the nursery, a cute little Thai girl, perhaps just 3 years old, was slowly, tragically going blind. It was a first sign indicating that her body was dying of HIV. To ease her pain, a female care worker held the sweet girl in her arms, the child's face visible just over the volunteer's shoulders. Thoughtfully, and respectfully, I recorded footage of her frail limbs swaying back and forth, being embraced, comforted and loved. Not a word was said by me, nor did I make the smallest sound. The dying little girl's tender moment became mine too. I can still see her innocent face in my mind as I write these words. She died only a few weeks later.

NIGER: In Niamey, during a visit to the city's Central Mosque, I was suddenly befriended by an assistant imam. When he discovered I was from America, and was a documentary director who was there to shoot cultural scenes of this dusty sub-Saharan city, he insisted straightaway on giving me a personally guided tour himself. Holding my hand, he walked our group to the exact spot up front where the president of the country worshipped each Friday at noon. We moved on to the exquisite paintings on the elaborate walls, the priceless carpets on the vast floor, and then observed a small group studying their Korans in the heart of the mosque.

I was respectful to him and listened to his eloquent, animated stories and observations. With previous experience in Africa, I knew that with his holding my hand that he now considered me - based on African customs and traditions between men - a new, dear friend. His holding my hand didn't bother me at all or make me nervous.

Later, after his guided tour of the grand building, I quietly asked for his permission to take video of the Koran study group. He said yes, it would be his and their honor. So, I was able to shoot some of the best Muslim prayer footage I have ever recorded in my career, even having the caretakers open the grand mosque windows and doors to allow for more light.

If I had been rude to the assistant imam, been upset at his holding my hand, or seemed in a careless, impatient hurry, I would never have won his trust, nor received his kind permission to photograph the Koran study group.

IVORY COAST: In upcountry Ivory Coast, we stopped at a local village to shoot a typical tribal scene. Before we pulled even one piece of equipment or bag from our vehicles, our colleagues and crew first went and met with the tribal chief. Soft drinks were offered, we sat in his small home, were welcomed, talked about the prosperity of the village, how his family and he were doing. We discussed the nature of our project, and what we might like to accomplish that morning, talked about what the chief thought might be permitted.

Then, and only then, did we ask his kind permission to film in his village and with his people. The chief (who was in his 30s) pulled out all the stops, asking the elderly, the children, the men and women, to put on village dress for our cameras. We recorded young girls pounding corn for the daily meal. Little children playing with makeshift toys. Old men playing checkers on the porch. Workers of every age gathering crops in the field. Kids collecting water.

Taking time to honor the chief, and involving him in the process, showed the proper respect for his leadership, and the local culture and people.

Walk softly, carry a small camera and wait for the right moment.

•

ADVICE

Here is what I can tell you on certain cultural subjects. There is probably much more trapped somewhere in the cobwebs of my brain. But know that I come by these opinions, ideas and experiences through learning - mostly - the hard way. That includes a range of successes, mistakes, observations and pitfalls.

BEING A FOREIGNER: There is no experience quite like being a small minority in someone else's country. Over time I've come to appreciate other views, beliefs, systems, languages and faiths of various, diverse nationalities and cultures. Relax, it's time to try another country for a change.

Travel is a great teacher, one of the best.

So let your journeys educate and enlighten you. Chances are, you'll not only come back a better person, but will have a greater appreciation of the many freedoms and luxuries available to you where you already live. Let these new experiences stretch and form you. You'll become a better person for it, inside and out.

TIME: Take your time. Don't sweat the little things. Westerners are far too often in an terrible hurry. Slow down, savor the moment and enjoy the ride. Know that time has different meanings in various cultures. So enjoy the differences and go with the flow. If you try too hard to bend people's concept of time, they - or probably you - will break.

THANK YOU: I have counted it up, and in my estimation I can say the two words *Thank You* in around 22 languages, including Finnish and Swahili. In some cases - like Nepalese, Hungarian and Romanian - it's the only phrase I know. But there is not a more important phrase than *Thank You. Please* is not bad either. *Hello. How are you? Good-bye.* Just a few key words learned can transform a person's stern face into a smiling one.

In almost any part of the world or any culture, your attempt to speak at least a few words of their local language will bring you some respect and appreciation. You are attempting to communicate in their native language, not yours. Sure, you may mess up your pronunciation. Or call someone a "pig's butt" when you meant to say "how beautiful your children are." But laugh, be humble, attempt to be polite and kind. You'll get through it somehow, someway. Bring a phrase book with you or ask someone local to help you with a few basic, key words.

PROPER LANGUAGE: Even when you share a common language, finding out the correct words that a country and culture employs, and using them in the right context, can only assist you in your travels. I mean, you can ask all day in London in the American dialect which way to the elevator, but saying where's *the lift* will do the job better. In France, an airport luggage cart is called a *chariot* (char-ee-oh). In Ireland, everything is *lovely*, In England, it's *splendid* or *brilliant*. Finding and using the local idioms (even slang, but be careful there) will assist you. Pay attention. Listen to waiters, clients, taxi drivers, the hotel front desk. And don't be afraid to ask the concierge for a smart phrase or two to help you too. People love to help. Just ask nicely, and choose wisely.

SMILING: The power of a smile is infectious. Many times I have walked into villages where they have never seen a fair-skinned person before, especially someone as white me. Babies go screaming into the bush or running back to their mother's arms. Countries are called to war. Drums start beating. There is a shrill call for revolution. Armies are formed. Even if the village elders may be closely looking you up and down, or that crowded cantina that you've run into to find a bathroom quickly may be sizing you up (good or bad) - *smile.* It makes a huge difference. (Remember, if you are a male to be careful about smiling at an unmarried female. They may consider it impolite and a sexual advance. But for 90% of the rest of the time, show some teeth.)

HUMOR: I am naturally funny by nature, enjoy a great joke and love to laugh. But what is funny to me may not have them rolling in the aisles in Cairo. Or Cape Town. Or Calcutta. Choose your moments for humor wisely. Pick the right situation and circumstances. Consider your audience. Humor can lead to very awkward moments, especially if your joke might be considered crude or offensive. Yes, humor can ease tension. But it also might start a small cross border war. Think twice before telling that old, reliable joke about the rabbi, the priest and the imam who had only one parachute as the airplane was going down.

And no matter what, stay away from the topics of politics, religion and sex. Period.

RELIGION: Be kind and courteous when touring churches, mosques, synagogues, temples and any houses of worship. Wearing the appropriate clothing (male or female) is a sign of respect, including the covering of heads, bare arms and legs. Learn the customs, including when to remove shoes, how to bow or kneel, and proper ways to shake hands (right hand only).

Making wise cracks about icons, paintings, statues, idols, holy books, music, services or any other aspect of a country's religious beliefs is disrespectful and callous. Many houses of worship are also historical points of interest, representing a cultural significance that goes far beyond just a place to pray. So try to consider how important the fascinating, majestic building you're visiting represents for a specific country, its people and their faith.

SAMPLE THE FOOD: In the chapter on Travel I mentioned the great joy I've had eating memorable meals in exotic places. And, naturally, some of that intriguing cuisine has come back later to haunt me. Then again, I once contracted terrible food poisoning from a tainted Rueben sandwich at a local Denny's in Santa Cruz, CA. So distance and exoticness aren't required for a bad tummy.

Try the local delicacies, get out there and taste what a country and culture have to offer. Nothing ventured, nothing gained. Get out of the hotel and go have a meal where the concierge suggests. Or ask around. See, experience, taste.

GETTING TO THE POINT: In many cultures, it is insincere and impolite to get straight to your point in any introductory conversation. This includes business, negotiating and production. Tea, coffee or a cold drink will be served first, as a sign of hospitality. Often, conversations begin with news about people's families, hobbies, your trip and points of interest. In fact, asking about a person's family, and how they are doing, is a great ice breaker. Get to know a person first before diving to the heart of why you are there or what you want. The grand plan of "bottom line" can wait until informal conversation and polite pleasantries are exchanged.

Start with the relationship first, expect the results to come later.

•

TOURIST OR TRAVELER?

Pushy, rude, loud and demanding behavior gets few people anywhere successfully in their own country. So, it probably won't work in a foreign country either. Learn to dial it down, or expect to head back to the airport soon.

You have a choice: tourist or traveler. If you view a foreign location as dirty, crowded, ill-tempered, slow and in a serious need of a big vacuum cleaner, you probably are a *tourist*. You'll return home complaining about how it rained, or the people couldn't understand a word you were saying. Griping about the traffic (try Mexico City or Bangkok sometime) accomplishes little. Being on the lookout for pizza or burgers everywhere you go spells tourist. Haggling and beating a vendor down to his or her very last drachma for the sport of it is embarrassing too.

However, if you love to taste new foods, experience colorful cultures, are flexible about time or schedules, easily converse with new people, and are willing to try out a few phrases in the local language, then there's a very good chance you are a *traveler*. I view travelers as white rice: people who take on and absorb the rich flavors of the many cultures, peoples and countries they've come into contact with.

Leave the attitudes, prejudices and preconceptions behind.

Become a traveler.

•

CALCUTTA, INDIA

My friend and colleague, Jaxn, related a story to me years back about a video shoot she had once done in Calcutta. She is a writer-producer, and was shooting a worthy children's literature project that goes into classrooms around the world and distributes inspirational books.

To shoot a promotional segment, her U.S.-based client had hired a local Indian video crew, including a camera man, sound man and director. But unless the director told the crew what to do, nothing happened. The director was essentially running the show, while ignoring his client, Jaxn. She found herself having little or no control over footage, shooting or logistics, despite her attempted input. The crew didn't furnish a video monitor, so unless Jaxn wanted to watch video playback on the camera's viewfinder, she had no way to confirm exactly what was being shot and recorded throughout the production day.

At the end, the shoot amounted to failed footage. Some of the cassettes turned out to be usable, but the sound was distorted on every cassette. To this day, she observes, she still doesn't know what the problem was - and didn't become aware that the footage was of such poor quality until she got home and viewed field tapes.

In retrospect, Jaxn found herself trapped inside a two fold dilemma: she was working with a crew with an Eastern mindset that basically wouldn't listen to their Western producer-client's input. Instead, the Indian director accomplished what *he* thought was appropriate for the shoot, his attitude being that he knew better.

Her challenges, at heart, also dealt with basic gender issues: men ignoring a female superior. Culture and communication walked hand-in-hand down the rough streets of Calcutta, and nothing but time and videotape were expended.

For filmmaking, respecting the culture can also mean understanding the truly vast differences that separate us, both on a personal level, and in our production or assignments. It's important - indeed necessary and vital - to get a real handle on the local culture you're seeing, experiencing and working within.

Can't get a grasp on how Thais work? Or why dinner for Argentines begins at 10 p.m.? Or why Germans love efficiency? My strong suggestion is to find and hire someone knowledgeable in-country who a) understands your goals, objectives and ways of production, and b) firmly understands the local culture, mindset, languages, customs and conditions well.

Listen to them, ask smart questions, understand their viewpoint...then find cultural consensus.

You are a guest in someone else's country. Act like one.

•

CULTURAL TACTICS FROM PROS

"Cultural faces have a powerful impact on the viewer. Much more than wide shots of locations. Shoot them at 60 fps for better impact."

- Steve Taylor, Digital Spatula

"Show local color. On trips abroad, show the cultural context by shooting marketplaces, landmark buildings, traffic, people on sidewalks, mosques and churches, etc. In the process try to include the sounds of music, people talking, traffic, etc."

- Stan Jeter, CBN News

"If you are going to be shooting outside of the USA, keep this in mind: Always remember you are a guest; i.e., don't expect everyone to act like an American. If you have the opportunity, learn the language. At least learn as many phrases as possible. Even if you struggle or mispronounce, people will appreciate that you respect them enough to try.

"I've found over the past 40+ years in the film/video business that most of the complaints about people in other countries come down to expecting the French, Spanish, Italians, or whomever, to be Americans and speak English. You will find that a little tolerance and a lot of planning will go a long way toward getting your production finished with the least amount of aggravation."

- Charley Buchanan, PBS cameraman

CHAPTER 16 REVIEW: CULTURE

1. Walk softly, carry a small camera and wait for the right moment.
2. Travel is a great teacher, one of the best.
3. Take your time. Don't sweat the little things.
4. Learn to say *Thank You* in the local language.
5. Stay away from the topics of politics, religion and sex. Period.
6. Start with the relationship first, expect results to come later.
7. Leave the attitudes, prejudices and preconceptions behind. Become a traveler.
8. You are a guest in someone else's country. Act like one.

CHAPTER 17: NO-NO'S

Taboos

•

"Fool me once, shame on you.

Fool me twice, shame on me."

- *Wise Old Saying*

Following is a basic list of Do's and Don'ts:

Promise only what you are confident you can deliver. Your word is valuable.

Showing up late to a shoot, flight or scheduled appointment can be a deal breaker.

Talking on your cell phone while setting up your next shoot - 60 seconds before going live-via-satellite - will get you fired and tossed off the show roster, forever.

Turn the cell phone off. Return or make calls *only* during an appropriate break.

Never steal another person's client or hand that person your business card.

If you receive a phone call or email for a shoot, assignment or project from your contractor's client, always refer them back to the original contractor who hired you. It's called *integrity*.

Never turn in work or projects for award consideration that do not belong to you, or for which you played only a minor, supporting role.

Share the credit. Praise other people's accomplishments before your own.

Pay people and vendors on time. If your client has not paid you yet, or anticipated funds haven't arrived, let others know soon. Keeping people in the communications loop makes a big difference.

Drugs. Don't.

Sex. Are you kidding? Don't.

Alcohol. Consider the consequences, setting, present company and your well being.

Wrap party. Leave early. Go back to your hotel room or go home. Remember that nothing good ever happens after midnight.

Don't throw someone else under the bus of blame when it's really your fault. Own up to your mistakes.

Gossip and rumors are like playing with matches in dry brush. What they start spreads fast.

Jet lag can turn you into a walking zombie. Don't get snippy. Rest, acclimate, adjust.

Cover your arms and legs (and head) when entering houses of worship. It's called *respect*.

Never yell at a gate agent, ticket counter rep, customs official or passport control officer. They have the power to have you wait forever...and to make your life miserable.

Don't call people above you, initially, by their first names. Until the ground rules are set, or a familiarity has developed that is understood, politely call them by their formal names.

Make sure people can find and reach you whenever possible.

Regarding grooming, bathing and washing habits: Look and smell good. Maintain proper hygiene. Wear clean clothes both outside and underneath. This should be a no brainer.

Watch your behavior, for your actions might turn into a misdemeanor or felony these days (that affects others too).

Hostile work environment. Don't threaten, demean or be violent with anyone.

Sexual harassment or lewdness. Back off, back away and change your attitude...fast.

Choose your words wisely. This includes jokes, crude or racial remarks and profanity.

Manipulation, pettiness and condescension are terrible traits.

Control your temper.

Don't bump into the lights or knock over the camera.

Be truthful on your invoice, time card, receipts and with your expense report.

Stow the negativity, criticism, sarcasm and toxicity at the door.

Don't keep talking about yourself and your abilities to anyone and everyone who will listen. Your work should speak for itself, and what talents you have will be evident and recognizable eventually.

Having a healthy sense of humor lightens the mood, but flippancy destroys it.

Reliability and trustworthiness are wonderful virtues - make them yours.

Work hard. Be positive, pleasant and likable. People at all levels will want to work with you again...and again.

Learn and excel at your craft. Your talents and dedication will certainly pay dividends.

•

WHEN THINGS GO FROM BAD TO WORSE

Bad client, producer and crew behavior on a shoot used to be tolerated decades ago, but now it can cost a production real time, money, embarrassment and a trip to the lawyer's office, the local jail, Superior Court or the morgue.

I worked on a show that had four hostile workplace lawsuits pending all at one time. One of the Executive Producers was constantly having to attend legal depositions.

Another TV series I know of discovered very late in the process that their art director had a serious drug problem. Because their production was just days from kicking off - crunch time - they banned the art director from working in the office, but kept a string of runners bringing him documents and props to his home. The staff muddled through to complete the series, but the art director was let go soon thereafter.

One crew member I heard of on a network series got drunk at a bar one night in a foreign land and punched another customer. The next day he was fired, given a one-way plane ticket, taken to the airport and sent home.

I followed another producer on a series who had just been fired for hostile workplace environment issues involving his production coordinator. Yet the show leadership was still trying to find various ways to farm freelance work to him because he was "so brilliant."

A major production company I worked for hired a new Supervising Producer for one of its benchmark TV series. After so many weeks, they found that virtually nothing was getting done with hiring and assignments. Then they discovered that the producer was spending his time in their production office writing a screenplay for another client. Fired.

A respected cameraman colleague and I were on a major shoot to East Africa. It was our first time to work together. What the ad agency didn't tell me was that he had a terrible drinking problem that reared its ugly head from time-to-time. Both in an African capital city, and the European stopover, he showed signs of getting inebriated at dinner, but stopped short. In the end, it was on the long transatlantic flight home to the USA where things went from bad to worse - he got drunk and belligerent on the plane. Finally, when he had passed out, I went to get some fresh air and walk to the back galley to tell the flight attendants to stop serving him alcohol. We never worked together again, thankfully.

I had a cameraman colleague try to reschedule meeting up with me overseas (with my camera gear) for a confirmed, scheduled shoot because he found that he could make a little more money by staying an extra couple days in Europe on another side project. He pleaded with me to arrive late to the Africa shoot. I said "no," that we had a commitment to keep.

One very talented cameraman I knew quite well had the phone number of my client, and got himself booked - independent of my company - on numerous overseas gigs, eventually stealing the client.

There was a cameraman who didn't like our group's camera gear who quietly started convincing our commercial client to go with a different camera package - his. Extra money in his pocket.

I can describe for you an award-winning sitcom director who was working on a series of infomercials where I ran camera. He announced to the client that he was wondering if - next time - the producers could hire a "better" camera crew. Sure enough, next shoot our excellent crew was replaced by a much more *expensive* camera team - all friends of the director. They had complained to him about their not getting enough freelance bookings. Quality and price weren't the issue - cronyism was.

A husband/wife editing team I worked with extensively - who lost scores of future bookings from me later - quietly started doing side shoots and projects for my main client without my knowledge.

There was the female editor who breast-fed her infant during an edit session (with client present) rather than our all taking a 15 minute break for the baby. Awkward. And unprofessional.

Editing a project at a major edit suite on a Saturday, the videotape operator could be loudly heard over the phone in the back of the room laying down bets on that day's college football games with his bookie.

One show I know of had a wrap party so loud, obnoxious and drunken that the *Hyatt Hotel* had to shut them down at 3 a.m. one night because of numerous guest complaints.

"From bad to worse" comes down, time and again, to both personal behavior and professional ethics...or lack thereof.

Do the right, honorable thing, show up on time, do your job well, keep your nose clean, stay away from dangerous vices (sex, anger, language, theft, drugs, alcohol), stay true to your word and any agreements, and don't steal someone else's client - you'll do just fine.

•

TABOO TACTICS FROM PROS

"NEVER tell a director or director of photography a shot is IMPOSSIBLE!! - try to do the shot a slightly different way to make it work, and see if they prefer that, or you can come to a mutual compromise."

- Michael J. Denton, network cameraman

"Never leave your master tapes in a rental car trunk...and then remember as your plane is taking off. Never happened to me, just saying."

- Paul Louis Cole, Compass Direct

"Here's one: don't lose your cool in front of cast and crew. Contrary to popular belief, a ranting and raving director DOES NOT inspire confidence in his creative collaborators, not does he/she help them to do their best creative work."

- Saqib Siddik, filmmaker

"No children, animals or fire on the set."

- Jon D. Smith, TV producer

"Only do deferred productions because it's someone you really want to work with, the cause is important to you, you get to travel somewhere cool, or you get the chance to work with a piece of equipment or use a technique you've been itching to try. NOT for any expectation of future payment. Do it for a reason that's important to you RIGHT NOW."

- Steven Bradford, Seattle Film Institute

CONCLUSION

It's a Wrap

•

Hopefully, a new concept, a practical suggestion, a creative idea or a solid tip you've learned in *Commando Tactics* will have you better prepared for your next project. Along the way, we've certainly discovered a few wonderful, memorable principles:

"A confident, relaxed director - who knows exactly what he or she wants and has communicated their vision properly - should be the calmest person on almost any set. "

"Where is the light?"

"Every camera move should have a reason."

"Time is either your best friend...or your worst enemy."

"Tell me a story."

"If you tell a compelling story, they will watch."

"What's your story about? What's it REALLY about?"

"If you don't communicate, you've got a dead shark on your hands."

"Facts go right to the head, but emotions go straight to the heart."

"A goal without a plan is just a wish."

"Get organized."

"No script? Changing/evolving script? Create a Pyramid Shot List."

"The best questions often come from the previous answer."

"Adapt. Overcome. Improvise."

"Good. Fast. Cheap. Pick two."

"No matter the size of your shoot, create a budget."

"Know your tools."

"Correct decisions in the field will continually serve you...and your project."

"Never enough time to do it *right*, but always enough time to do it *wrong*!"

"Using talented people should not be considered a luxury or rarity, but a basic necessity. "

"*Show* me *most* of the time. *Tell* me *some* of the time."

"Garbage in, garbage out. Same adage applies to sound."

"Things always change. Bank on it."

"Explanation is fine, but it's imagination that sparks the fire. "

"Being well prepared cuts down on anxiety!"

"Don't skimp on finding the best person for on-camera duties."

"Did you bring the *Spinelli Lens*?"

If you put into play at least one or two of this book's tactics anytime soon, then we've been pretty successful together in this endeavor.

Good shooting.

CRAIG D. FORREST

Over a 30+ year professional producing & directing career, Craig's television and documentary projects have taken him to 144 countries, flown him 14x around-the-world and also landed him on 6 continents. Over 200 overseas assignments have flung him into dangerous hot spots like Iraq, Cuba, Sri Lanka, Burundi, the Congo, El Salvador, Palestine, Cambodia, Uganda, Haiti, Burma, Chad & Bosnia.

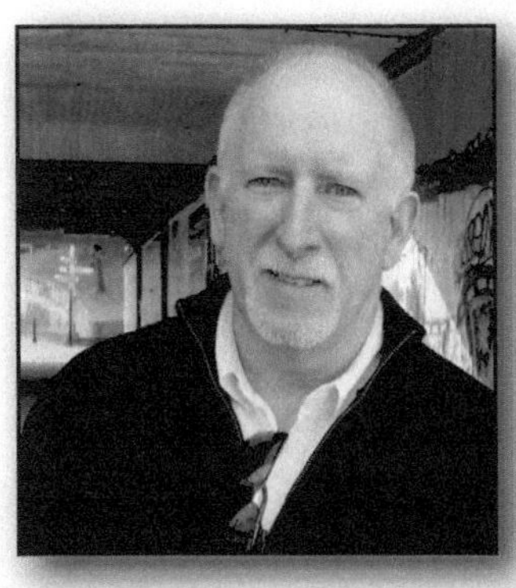

His work has won 29 tv, film, video & festival awards, including a *Cine Golden Eagle*, plus multiple *Telly*, *Aurora*, *Videographer*, *Aegis* and *Communicator* trophies. Craig was part of the production team for *The Amazing Race* (Season 14), which won the 2009 *Primetime Emmy* for *Outstanding Reality Competition* program.

Notable clients have included *CBS*, *ABC*, *Discovery Channel*, *HBO*, *Travel Channel*, *UPN*, *Animal Planet*, *PBS*, *Warners Bros*, *A&E*, *Fox Sports*, *AMC*, *Univision*, *Billy Graham*, *World Vision*, *Far East Broadcasting*, *Latin America ChildCare*, *OneHope*, *Hyatt Hotels*, *DuPont*, *Toshiba*, *Northwest Airlines*, *Memorex*, *Nestlé*, *Infiniti*, *Wells Fargo* and *McDonald's*.

Craig holds a Masters degree in Film Studies from the *Conservatory of Motion Pictures* at *Chapman University*, and a Bachelors in Theology from *Bethany University*.

A voting member of the *Academy of Television Arts & Sciences* (Emmys), he also holds membership in the prestigious *Travelers' Century Club* (100+ countries). Most recently, Craig has served as an Adjunct Professor of Media Production at *Pepperdine University* in Malibu, CA.

He is also the author of *The Influence of Alexander Mackendrick on the Kailyard Film Sub-genre* (VDM Verlag). Craig's next book will be *Night Train to Cairo: A Filmmaker's Journey Across the Globe*.

www.ingramcontent.com/pod-product-compliance
Lightning Source LLC
Chambersburg PA
CBHW020745180526
45163CB00001B/354

* 9 7 8 0 6 1 5 4 9 5 4 7 7 *